BUILDING MENNONITE BELONGING

Building Mennonite Belonging

TOWARD AN INTERCULTURAL CHURCH

HYUNG JIN (PABLO) KIM SUN

McGill-Queen's University Press
Montreal & Kingston | London | Chicago

ISBN 978-0-2280-2389-0 (paper)
ISBN 978-0-2280-2390-6 (ePDF)
ISBN 978-0-2280-2391-3 (ePUB)

Legal deposit first quarter 2025
Bibliothèque nationale du Québec

Printed in Canada on acid-free paper that is 100% ancient forest free (100% post-consumer recycled), processed chlorine free

This book has been published with the help of a grant from the Federation for the Humanities and Social Sciences, through the Awards to Scholarly Publications Program, using funds provided by the Social Sciences and Humanities Research Council of Canada.

Funded by the Government of Canada | Financé par le gouvernement du Canada | Canada | Canada Council for the Arts | Conseil des arts du Canada

We acknowledge the support of the Canada Council for the Arts.

Nous remercions le Conseil des arts du Canada de son soutien.

McGill-Queen's University Press in Montreal is on land which long served as a site of meeting and exchange amongst Indigenous Peoples, including the Haudenosaunee and Anishinabeg nations. In Kingston it is situated on the territory of the Haudenosaunee and Anishinaabek. We acknowledge and thank the diverse Indigenous Peoples whose footsteps have marked these territories on which peoples of the world now gather.

Library and Archives Canada Cataloguing in Publication

Title: Building Mennonite belonging : toward an intercultural church / Hyung Jin Kim Sun.
Names: Kim Sun, Hyung Jin, author
Description: Includes bibliographical references and index.
Identifiers: Canadiana (print) 20240439147 | Canadiana (ebook) 20240439198 | ISBN 9780228023890 (paper) | ISBN 9780228023906 (ePDF) | ISBN 9780228023913 (ePUB)
Subjects: LCSH: Mennonite Church Canada. | LCSH: Mennonites—Canada. | LCSH: Multiethnic churches—Canada. | LCSH: Church and minorities—Canada. | LCSH: Multiculturalism—Canada.
Classification: LCC BX8121.3 .K56 2025 | DDC 289.7/71—dc23

This book was designed and typeset by Garet Markvoort in 11/14 Sina Nova with Gotham. Copyediting by Ryan Perks.

To my Mennonite mentors, including the late David Augsburger, Wilbert Shenk, and Gary Harder whose wisdom continues to guide me long after our time together. To Michele Rae Rizoli, Lydia Harder, and John Roth, who accepted me just as I am and encouraged me to continue sharing my voice.

To my Mennonite siblings who embraced me as "full Mennonite."

And to all within the global Anabaptist-Mennonite community who strive for full belonging: you are the edge walkers and the visionaries who are leading Anabaptist-Mennonite churches toward becoming healthier and more beautifully complex intercultural communities. Your wisdom and struggles have not only profoundly shaped me – they have also inspired the creation of this book.

CONTENTS

ACKNOWLEDGMENTS

My deepest gratitude goes to my academic mentors, Thomas Reynolds, Jeremy Bergen, and Néstor Medina, whose unwavering guidance and wisdom have laid the foundation of my research journey. I am profoundly thankful as well to my wife, Jinah Im, for her endless support and patience, which have been indispensable to the completion of this work.

I also extend my appreciation to the Institute for the Study of Global Anabaptism and to Mennonite Church Canada for their invaluable support and encouragement throughout the development of this book. Special thanks to Kyla Madden and the entire editorial team at McGill-Queen's University Press for their meticulous attention and dedication, crucial in bringing this book to publication.

Additionally, I am grateful to my colleagues, especially Adrian Jacobs, Jonathan Schmidt, and Dorothy Pang, whose work and enriching conversations have deepened and broadened my understanding of intercultural engagement. Your insights have been invaluable.

This work is a testament to the collaborative spirit and collective wisdom of many. To each of you, I offer my eternal gratitude.

ABBREVIATIONS

AMBS	Anabaptist Mennonite Biblical Seminary
BIPOC	Black, Indigenous, and people of colour
LGBTQAI2+	lesbian, gay, bisexual, transgender, queer and/or questioning, asexual, intersex, two-spirit, and many others
MCC	Mennonite Central Committee
MC Canada	Mennonite Church Canada
MCC Canada	Mennonite Central Committee Canada
MCEC	Mennonite Church Eastern Canada
MC USA	Mennonite Church USA
SPT	shalom political theology
TRC	Truth and Reconciliation Commission of Canada

BUILDING MENNONITE BELONGING

INTRODUCTION

I am a Mennonite. I was born and raised in Asunción, Paraguay, by a Korean immigrant family. Living in Paraguay, I often heard about Mennonites, and even visited the Mennonite colony of "Filadelfia" several times to see how Mennonites lived as a community. Despite my frequent encounters with Mennonites in Paraguay, it never occurred to me that Mennonites were religious people. It was only when I went to Fuller Theological Seminary in Pasadena, California, that I discovered Mennonites were part of the Christian faith. While at Fuller, I met a number of Mennonite professors and colleagues, and through them, I felt a strong attraction to the Mennonite faith. Indeed, after attending a Korean Mennonite church for a year, I decided to join the larger Mennonite family out of a desire to be a better disciple of Jesus.

However, once I began to attend Mennonite regional and national gatherings in the United States, I returned time and again from those meetings feeling uneasy. More often than not, when I arrived at those gatherings it was immediately evident that the majority of Mennonites there were white. Then, when I began greeting people, they soon started playing "the Mennonite game," making family connections within a network of genealogical connections. Later, during our lunchtime, I got to hear about Mennonite foods like zwieback, vareniki, and borscht, which are dishes that generally fall in the category of Polish, Ukrainian, and/or Russian cuisine. Once the events were over and it was time for me to travel back home, I was not sure if I attended a church gathering or a cultural gathering. Throughout my involvement with the Mennonite Church, I have learned that Mennonites form both an ethnic and a faith community. In the faith community that holds on to particular ethnic identities, I, as a Paraguayan of Korean descent, felt that I would never be "Mennonite" enough.

After this realization, I had three options: either leave the denomination, stay and try to assimilate as much as possible, or invite the church to become a community that would fully embrace people from different racial, ethnic, and cultural backgrounds. I did not want to leave the denomination because I deeply agree with Mennonite confessions of faith and because I had already built strong relationships with numerous church members. At the same time, I did not want to assimilate myself to the predominant culture because my ethnocultural identities are core to who I am, and giving up on them would mean rejecting an important part of me. As a result, I chose to stay and join the movement to encourage the church to be a critical intercultural community so that people like me can experience full belonging. And this book is my small contribution to the work of pushing the church to become what many of us hope it to be.

Some might argue that Mennonites cannot form an intercultural church because, unlike in other Christian denominations like Baptists, Methodist, and the United Church of Canada, members of this denomination have a strong connection to their ethnic identities. However, while acknowledging the complex interplay of faith, ethnicity, culture, and race, I firmly believe that the Mennonite Church can indeed be transformed into an intercultural community. Its theological foundations promoting inclusivity, its longstanding traditions of hospitality, and its history of facing persecution inspire members to embrace marginalized communities.

Furthermore, the current composition of the church's membership is more diverse and global than ever before. While there may still be churches situated in rural areas whose leaders argue against intercultural adaptation due to a lack of ethnic and racial diversity among their congregants, a closer examination of these congregations often reveals hidden diversity. Even within seemingly homogenous communities, individuals of mixed-race heritage or belonging to racialized groups may go unnoticed, especially when their appearance suggests they are white, a dynamic referred to as "white-presenting" or "white-passing." Upon closer scrutiny, it often becomes evident that a rural church's community is more diverse than initially perceived.

Another crucial question to consider is whether our church remains homogenous because our surrounding neighbourhoods are predominantly white, or if it is because we primarily welcome people who resemble us. Canadian society has become significantly more diverse over the past decade – a trend that is set to continue. Statistics Canada projects that by 2041, the Black, Indigenous, and people of colour (or BIPOC) population could make up between 43.6 and 49.8 per cent of the total Canadian population.[1] This means that in less than twenty years, one in two people will be non-white, and these demographic changes will also manifest in rural areas. As a result, even if local rural churches currently appear homogenous, there are compelling reasons for them to engage in the dialogue about becoming more intercultural.

Yet, while the Mennonite Church may be heading in this direction, increasing diversity is in itself insufficient since there remain significant barriers to the development of a truly intercultural community. Perhaps most importantly, it has failed to offer a robust vision of what an intercultural Mennonite Church would look like in the current context and what changes are required to strive toward that aim. Allow me to portray further the complexity of Mennonite identities, and both the potential benefits and challenges of becoming an intercultural Mennonite Church in greater detail.

An Anabaptist group that began in Europe in the sixteenth century, Mennonites have moved around to different parts of the world through migration and missionary endeavours. The earliest wave of Mennonite settlement in Canada occurred between 1786 and 1836. From their initial settlement in this country through the present day, Mennonites have become "a transformed people"[2]: they have learned how to hold on to the core Anabaptist-Mennonite beliefs and practices while adjusting to and engaging with the modern Canadian setting. During their early establishment, Mennonite groups were mostly composed of white Europeans from Swiss, German, Dutch, and Russian backgrounds, and they lived separate from mainstream society – geographically and socio-politically – in order to maintain their particular identity. This intentional nonconformity and willingness to live as separate people was rooted in Mennonites' theological commitment and history of persecution.[3] However, as they endured two world wars and experienced social changes such as modernization, urbanization, and the drastic increase of immigrants from non-European countries, most Mennonites accommodated themselves to these cultural changes, became more keenly involved in society, and welcomed people from diverse cultural backgrounds. Furthermore, Anabaptist-Mennonite churches have become much more global; as of 2022, 69.5 per cent of Mennonites worldwide resided in Africa, Latin America, and Asia,[4] and since 2001, 93 per cent of the growth in the church has come from these continents.[5]

While the church has become much more global and diverse, the principle Mennonite ethnic identities, particularly Swiss, German, Dutch, and Russian, are still dominant within it; as a result, people who are not part of these ethnicities experience barriers to being fully integrated into church life, and they express frustration at being considered mere "half-Mennonites."[6] They also name whiteness as another barrier that excludes them, since it is associated with the dominant Mennonite ethnicities.

The discussion around ethnicity and faith within the Mennonite circle is not new. In the article "The Poetics of Peoplehood: Ethnicity and Religion among Canada's Mennonites," Royden Loewen, a Canadian Mennonite historian, outlines this discourse quite well. He presents six ways that Mennonite groups deal with and position themselves vis-à-vis ethnicity and faith: (1) embracing ethnicity while de-emphasizing religious tradition (people who no longer identify as Mennonites in religious terms); (2) accepting Mennonite ethnicity while disdaining traditional Mennonite religiousness (Mennonites linked to overtly Canadian evangelicalism); (3) separating ethnicity from religious faith and fully supporting Mennonite faith while trying to push Mennonite ethnicity aside (Neo-Anabaptist); (4) linking Mennonite faith and Mennonite ethnicity (Old Order, or conservative rural, Mennonites); (5) recognizing that Mennonite ethnicity is symbolic and without religious significance, while seeming to exist almost naturally alongside Mennonite religious faith (a large majority of Mennonites); and (6) identifying as Mennonite but not as a Mennonite ethnicity or with Anabaptist faith (self-identifying Mennonites for reasons of friendship, gratitude, and even a strategy of integrating into a highly respected social sector of middle-class Canada).[7] Loewen clarifies that there are, of course, many more diverse responses beyond those articulated in his article. And, as his outline of the discourse on Mennonite faith and ethnicity demonstrates, it is highly likely that questions around faith and ethnicity will persist, and that the majority of Mennonites in both Canada and the United States will continue to view the ethnic aspect as crucial to their identity. This is problematic because emphasizing Mennonite "ethnicities" privileges the "foundational" ethnicities, those cultural and historical traditions whose ancestry is linked directly to what is seen as "originary" Mennonite traditions with European roots. As a result, willingly or unwillingly, "ethnic" Mennonites create and maintain an "us versus them" dynamic within Mennonite churches, where "we" are the "hosts," and "they" are the perpetual "guests." Collapsing religious and ethnic identities into a single meaning, as if being Mennonite necessarily means being of European descent, will exclude non-dominant groups and ensure they are not considered "full" Mennonites. Even though Mennonite churches are becoming locally and globally more diverse, in accordance with Mennonites' commitment and calling, many non-ethnic Mennonites are experiencing ongoing marginalization and exclusion. This reality is challenging Mennonites in Canada and the United States to re-examine issues of ethnicity, race, culture, and faith from a fresh perspective.

This issue is not exclusive to Canadian Mennonites. Scholars like Paul Bramadat and David Seljak observed that Christian churches in Canada were becoming notably more diverse, even within denominations originally founded by specific ethnic groups, such as the Scots in the Presbyterian Church, the English in the Anglican Church, the Germans in the Lutheran Church, the Dutch in the Christian Reformed Church, and others.[8] However, as has been the case with the Mennonites, this compositional diversity does not naturally translate into these churches becoming healthy intercultural communities where ethnic minority groups are fully embraced and celebrated. Consequently, the insights presented in this book are pertinent and valuable for Canadian churches deeply connected to specific ethnic identities, as they grapple with the challenges of navigating diversity, inclusion, and the intersection of faith, race, and ethnicity.

In this complex situation, a faithful and transformative response to these challenges for Mennonite Church Canada is to become a critical intercultural church that addresses the issues of faith, culture, ethnicity, and race in the Mennonite community; identifies exclusionary behaviours and practices within and outside the church; incorporates the voices and the experiences of marginalized people; and offers ways to live into its own historic peace church tradition and its missional identity in the current Canadian multicultural context. It is worth noting that my use of the term "critical" here underscores the importance of self-examination, critical thinking, and analysis in the journey toward becoming an intercultural church. This critical perspective will not only elucidate the necessity of churches embracing interculturality but will also outline the practical steps to do so.

Although the Bible does not use the term "intercultural," the idea and the aspiration are expressed throughout scripture: in the Creation story, God blesses the diversity of all creation; God diversifies languages to the people working toward uniformity, instead of unity, as they were building the Tower of Babel; God calls Israel to be a blessings to all nations; Jesus commissions his followers to make disciples of all ethnicities; Jesus's disciples preach in various languages on the day of Pentecost; the early church in the book of Acts works to be a more inclusive church starting from the Hellenistic Jews to the Gentile Christians; Paul teaches that the church needs to be inter-ethnic in Galatians and Ephesian, etc.. Another example, and one that resonates strongly with me, is Revelation 7:9–12. In this passage, a great multitude of people from all nations, tribes, and ethnicities is on the march. With their own languages, they are worshipping the Lamb and the one who sits on the throne. They praise with their own particular ethnocultural expressions, and God fully accepts their worship. This passage captures a beautiful vision of intercultural worship as a dynamic site of exchange where all beings are reconciled under God and people can fully be themselves, praising God in their own unique ways. It invites all Christians to strive and embody this vision with a firm conviction that God is working toward its fulfillment.

The effort to become an intercultural church is not only biblically sound: as I will examine in more depth in chapter 1, it is also a fundamental component of being more fully Mennonite. Anabaptist-Mennonite understandings of baptism and communion call the church to actively engage with differences and celebrate diversity in the body of Christ. God's vision of shalom, which is also integral to Mennonite beliefs, requires us to live in right relations with each other and to stand against any type of oppression and violence, such as racism, ethnocentrism, or sexism. Moreover, as a missional church, Mennonites are called to be an alternative community in society – and a key feature of this in current contexts involves being an inter-ethnic and interracial community in which everyone is fully accepted, respected, and loved. There are firm roots in biblically based Anabaptist-Mennonite theological perspectives for this emphasis on becoming a critical intercultural church.

From the outset, I differentiate between the concepts of multicultural and intercultural. The word "multicultural" is defined as "designating or pertaining to a society consisting of many culturally distinct groups," while "intercultural" means "taking place between cultures; belonging to or derived from different cultures."[9] "Multicultural" relates to diverse cultural groups coexisting together; it recognizes the existence of different cultural groups, but it does not examine how these groups interact among themselves. In comparison, "intercultural" designates a type of engagement between different cultural groups in which they not only tolerate each other, but actively interact with and influence each other as well. Yet, not every intercultural engagement is healthy and respectful. For this reason, the type of critical intercultural relationship that I am describing is an engagement based on love and justice with a clear understanding of the existing power dynamic within one's social context. Through this mutual interaction, people share cultural aspects, broaden their understanding of God, deepen their life of discipleship and community, and strive for a fair distribution of power among all parties, so that there can be equity and justice for all. Particularly in the Canadian context, to be a critical intercultural church means to be a decolonizing and anti-racist community because Canada was established through settler colonialism and is built upon the ideology of white supremacism. Indeed, both of these isms are still deeply engrained in Canadian society and ideas of Canadian nationhood. These concepts and more will be unpacked in the following chapters.

In essence, the "critical intercultural" descriptor signifies a deliberate and deep commitment to fostering diversity, inclusivity, and justice. This approach entails self-examination, critical thinking, and active engagement with various cultural groups, all in an attempt to cultivate a community where individuals engage with one another, demonstrate mutual respect, and address exclusionary practices. Rooted in biblical principles and the church's mission, it places a strong emphasis on social justice, equitable interactions, and the inclusion of marginalized voices. Additionally, it acknowledges the imperative of decolonization and anti-racism in the Canadian context as a means to challenge oppressive historical systems and work toward a more inclusive and equitable society that values and empowers all cultural groups.

Recognizing that one cannot cover everything, I've limited the scope of my analysis in the following ways. First, the book focuses only on the Mennonites who hold up their religious identity as a fundamental marker of their community. In other words, this research does not seek to examine those Mennonites who distance themselves from religious identity and consider themselves only "ethnically" or "culturally" Mennonite. Second, Mennonite groups in Canada are diverse, with the majority being concentrated in Ontario and Manitoba; significant populations are also found in Saskatchewan, Alberta, and British Columbia. Denominationally, there are approximately thirty different conferences or fellowships within the Anabaptist-Mennonite tradition in Canada. As of 2020, the four largest are the Canadian Conference of Mennonite Brethren (with 34,693 members), Mennonite Church Canada (with 26,000 members), the Hutterian Brethren Church (with 14,900 members), and the Old Colony Mennonite Church (with 13,778 members).[10] For the purpose of this study, the primary focus will be on Mennonites affiliated with Mennonite Church Canada (MC Canada) denomination, which was formed through the merger of two binational conferences: the General Conference Mennonite Church and the Mennonite Church. This integrated entity subsequently divided into two national bodies, MC Canada and Mennonite Church USA (MC USA). The Mennonites under examination in this study are structurally affiliated with MC Canada, and they adhere to a common statement of faith known as *Confession of Faith in a Mennonite Perspective*. It is important to clarify that this book does not outline specific steps for MC Canada, as a denominational organization, to pursue systemic change. Instead, it offers guidelines, resources, insights, and the theological imagination necessary to help Canadian Mennonite churches on their journey toward becoming intercultural communities. It does not aim to provide concrete recommendations for the administrative offices of MC Canada. Third, my analysis of the Canadian context is not comprehensive in the sense of covering multicultural histories and policies, nor do I address settler-colonial legacies in detail, as other studies have already done these; however, I incorporate insights from these historical and social factors in this book, since they are instructive in developing the discussion, especially on how others are grappling with these differences.

In building the case for why and how MC Canada should become a critical intercultural church, the book is divided into three parts. In part 1, I begin with a descriptive examination of Canadian Mennonites' understanding of peoplehood. Fernando Enns differentiates between the "believed church" and "experienced church": the "believed church" is what a church should be and is called to be, and the "experienced church" is the church that people experience in a certain historical and social reality. This echoes the classic distinction between the church as a theological reality and as a sociological reality. Utilizing this concept, I analyze both the "believed" and the "experienced" church of Canadian Mennonites in order to arrive at a more appropriate and holistic understanding of the church.

In chapter 1, I compare three different theological views of the Mennonite Church – as messianic community, missional church, and shalom church – to offer a broader and more diverse view of "believed" Mennonite peoplehood. Widely accepted by Mennonites, these theological ideals show that Mennonites aspire to engage with the world, dialogue with those who hold different theological views as well as those from diverse ethnocultural backgrounds, work toward reconciliation, seek peace, and strive for social transformation. These commitments, beliefs, and aspirations are not only crucial aspects of becoming a critical intercultural church but are also distinctive Mennonite theo-ethical approaches.

In chapter 2, to analyze "experienced" Mennonite peoplehood, I survey historical accounts and sociological analyses of Mennonite identity, drawing primarily from a series of pathbreaking books that have already advanced this work, including *Mennonite Mosaic: Identity and Modernization* by Howard Kauffman and Leo Driedger, *Mennonite Peacemaking: From Quietism to Activism* by Leo Driedger and Donald Kraybill, and *Mennonite Society* by Calvin Redekop. I then explain how the concept of peoplehood and the view of missions have changed throughout the Mennonite Church's presence in Canada, especially in the context of modernization, urbanization, and other socio-historical factors. I further explain that, counter to the stereotypical depiction of Mennonites as closed off, they have in fact been actively engaging with the world, accommodating themselves to a drastically changing society without losing their Anabaptist-Mennonite tradition, and working to become a more global and diverse church. Yet, critical voices from within are raising issues of gender, race, and ethnicity and challenging the church to be more inclusive and welcoming so that the community can become truly transformed and faithfully live out the gospel of peace. At the end of chapter 2, I reiterate that there are theological resources, praxes, and lived experiences that are inviting Mennonite churches to become critically intercultural. But while such an aspiration certainly exists, it is still not clear how Mennonites can build a critical intercultural church in a situation where their religious identity is deeply tied to dominant ethnocultural and racial identities.

Part 2 investigates the concepts of culture, context, ethnicity, race, and faith, and the interconnections that exist between them, a basis for a discussion of how Mennonites can become a critical intercultural community in multicultural Canada (which is developed at greater length in part 3). Chapter 3 engages the work of contextual theologians such as Stephen Bevans, Néstor Medina, and Kathryn Tanner to highlight the intrinsic relationship between context and theology. Drawing on Stephen Bevans's six different models of contextual theology, I argue that the best of these Mennonite models can emerge through a contextual and liberative approach, which entails the combination of anthropological, praxis, and countercultural models. To further develop a nuanced and dialectical understanding of culture, ethnicity, and race as both informed by and informing theo-ethical perspectives, I incorporate insights from critical race theory and ethnocultural studies.

To situate this contextual and liberative work in a Canadian milieu, in chapter 4 I explain how ethnocultural and racial differences are managed and controlled through policies governing multiculturalism. The work of some critical social theorists reveals the degree to which Canadian multiculturalism is built on the principles of white supremacy and settler colonialism. These insights, coupled with the experiences of racialized people, challenge notions of Canadian multiculturalism and call for a different way to live in and engage with our diverse society. As I argue throughout the chapter, working toward a critical intercultural church is one example of this type of engagement. To be more specific, it means to be both decolonizing and anti-racist. Toward the end of the chapter,

I analyze further the concept of interculturality, noting how that term is used in different geographical locations and fields of study, including theology. This overview then helps to formulate a foundational principle of critical intercultural engagement from an Anabaptist-Mennonite perspective: shalom.

Building on part 1, and incorporating the critical analysis of culture, race, ethnicity, and faith in the Canadian context elaborated in part 2, I begin part 3 by critically reassessing the notion of Mennonite peoplehood from a contextual and liberative perspective in chapter 5. My aim here is to illuminate the material basis for particular guidelines on how Canadian Mennonites can become a critical intercultural church. By analyzing the sources, norms, and frames of three Mennonite theologies – messianic community, missional church, and shalom church – I identify five problematic issues in Mennonite theologies: (1) the sharp contrast between the church and world; (2) the belief that Jesus and the Bible are the final authority, while in reality relying on other theological sources without recognizing it; (3) a strong emphasis on Christology that dismisses the inclusive nature of God, Jesus, and the Holy Spirit; (4) the widespread acceptance of existing norms within the community, such as whiteness, patriarchy, and heteronormativity, which profoundly influence theological discourses; and (5) unconsciously assuming and being complicit in settler-colonial project. Furthermore, by reassessing the "experienced" church, I assert that "ethnic myopia" and "lax racial awareness" are preventing the church community from becoming a critical intercultural church that engages in decolonizing and anti-racism work. In light of this, I claim that, instead of dismissing the dominant Mennonite ethnicities, the church should recognize the multiple ethnicities present in its congregations and commit to working toward empowering marginalized groups to serve as full participants in the church who offer valuable contributions to Mennonite peoplehood.

As a vehicle for naming, resisting, and transforming these excluding practices and problematic issues, in chapter 6 I offer three theo-ethical norms: justice and love, hospitality, and mutuality, which together are embedded in the concept of shalom. With their intersecting themes, these norms form a kind of constellation capable of guiding the construction of a critical intercultural Mennonite Church in Canada. They invite us to work toward intercultural unity, practise radical discipleship and radical hospitality, strive for shalom and prophetic dialogue in multicultural publics, and seek repentance and reconciliation in Indigenous-settler relations.

PART ONE
Mennonite Ecclesiology

In order to propose how MC Canada can become a critical intercultural church, a descriptive analysis of the theology, history, and sociology of Canadian Mennonites and their place in contemporary Canadian society is required as a first step. Part 1 aims to do that by examining MC Canada as both a "believed" church and an "experienced" church, a dual concept borrowed from Fernando Enns. Briefly, "believed" church is the perception of what a church should be and is called to be, while "experienced" church is the lived experience of the church within a certain historical and social reality.[1] This echoes the classic distinction between the church as a theological reality and the church as a sociological reality.[2] It is crucial to examine both aspects so as to arrive at a holistic understanding of the Mennonite community. Sometimes the distinction between the "believed" and the "experienced" church may assume the appearance of a binary, but the two elements are actually interconnected. Some theologians who write about the "believed" church, like Malinda Berry (whose work will be examined more closely in chapter 1), seriously engage issues of power, privilege, and race because they want to ground their work and address problems they see in people's lived experiences. Then there are Mennonite sociologists like Leo Driedger and Donald Kraybill who write about the "experienced" church but also incorporate theological concepts into their work. Therefore, while it is important to distinguish between these two aspects, it is also crucial to remember that they are intertwined.

In an effort to examine both aspects of the church, part 1 is divided into two chapters. The first chapter begins by examining three different approaches to Mennonite ecclesiology – namely, the church as messianic, missional, and shalom – to develop a broader understanding of the "believed" church. I intentionally choose these three perspectives because their proponents have written extensively and because their theologies are different enough from each other to be compared and contrasted. By juxtaposing them, I am presenting a wide range of Mennonite ecclesiologies and the theological ideals that Mennonites already affirm. As I assess these theological perspectives, I note that the theological and practical bases for becoming an intercultural church are already present in Mennonite perspectives, though the term "intercultural" has not been used. In other words, my project is not additive – that is, offering materials external to Mennonite beliefs and practices that should be incorporated – but rather arises internally from the ferment of Mennonite principles and best practices, providing resources to address a changing context.

To comprehend the character of "experienced" Mennonite peoplehood, chapter 2 offers a survey of Mennonite historical accounts and sociological analyses. This demonstrates how the Mennonite concept of peoplehood, perspectives on difference and diversity, and engagement with the world have changed throughout Mennonites' historically negotiated presence in Canada. Building upon this, I comment on emerging tensions between the "believed" and the "experienced" church within MC Canada. While these tensions are problematic, I note that they can be harnessed productively to (1) further develop theologies that resonate with current contexts, and (2) offer theological aspirations for believers to live out their calling in concrete settings.

As a broad framework, I choose to compare the conceptions of the "believed" and the "experienced" church for two reasons. First, I seek to find ways to lessen the gap between the two perspectives. In one sense, this gap is inevitable because the church is both a theological reality (creedal, established by Christ, invisible, and eschatological) and a sociological reality (human, fallible, institutional, visible, and empirical). However, from an Anabaptist-Mennonite perspective, the church is called to strive to be a visible community of disciples, an eschatological community.[3] Furthermore, from a liberative view, Christians are to work toward a realized eschatology – actualizing God's work in the world – even as they recognize that the full manifestation of God's reign will be fulfilled in history's final event. For these reasons, and because of Jesus's call for us to live in community as disciples, being a faithful church entails narrowing the gap, at least as much as possible given the limitations of human nature and institutional frameworks. Hence, by bridging the "believed" and the "experienced" church, this project aspires to and works toward a theological reality fully realizable only in the future.

The second reason I make this comparison is to highlight the productive relationship between praxis and theology. According to liberation theologians, praxis and theology are intertwined, meaning that theology influences praxis and praxis shapes theology. Christians are committed to living out their faith and engaging in the praxis of liberation in a concrete socio-historical context of injustice and oppression. From these commitments and praxis, Christians critically reflect on their faith. This reflection is theology. Hence, as Gustavo Gutiérrez asserts, theology is a second act; that is, theological reflection is what comes in light of experience and action in concrete situations, as a means to engage more deeply toward liberative ends. This hermeneutic circle prioritizes the lived experience of injustice and oppression.[4] Based on this critical reflection and on other theological resources like the Bible, theology thus strives to enrich and empower the praxis and the commitment to liberation by explaining how God is already working in the world and how we as believers need to participate in this work.

In light of this insight, it is possible to see how the experiences (or praxes) of Canadian Mennonites have been shaping Mennonite theologies, and, conversely, how their theological frameworks have been helping them to reflect on their way of living. One salient example of this in the Mennonite perspective is the practice of nonconformity. Nonconformity, which was a commitment from the very beginning of the Anabaptist movement, was first considered a praxis connected to the belief that Canadian Mennonites should be separated from the societies surrounding them geographically, culturally, and politically in order to live out radical discipleship. However, as Mennonites faced several social changes that required engaging more fully in society, the praxis of nonconformity was diversified and diluted in some cases. As a result, this praxis broadened its theological conception, and it articulated a new meaning of praxis. Instead of thinking of nonconformity as geographical, cultural, and political separation, some Mennonites began to embrace the concept of ethical separation, in which one interacts with people from other communities while living out and maintaining different ethical standards than non-believers.[5] (I offer a fuller explanation of these various interpretations in chapter 2.) Hence, the "believed" church inspired the community to live out what they believe, and the "experienced" church informed their ecclesiology; the church incorporated insights and new understanding from people's experiences, so that the theological perspective might be empowering, relevant, and appropriate to the context. In the same way, my comparison of the experienced and the believed church may constructively shape Mennonite theologies and empower the lifestyles and praxes of Canadian Mennonites.

A note of clarification: Part 1 does not aim to cover the complex landscape of Mennonite history and sociology in Canada. It focuses instead on providing materials to facilitate a productive way of using the "believed" and "experienced" church to open up possibilities for becoming an intercultural church. In that sense, this section of the book focuses more on documenting and investigating several key moments of change in Mennonite identity, whereby Mennonites have renegotiated existing boundaries and navigated both inner and outer transformations, reacting and engaging theologically with difference and diversity. When I use the term "difference," I mean identity positions like gender, race, ethnicity, etc. Difference among people does not mean that there is no common ground or overlapping experience. Like Iris Marion Young says, different groups always have in some respects similar aspects, "and always potentially share some attributes, experiences, and goals."[6]

1

Believed Church: The Church as a Theological Reality

Like any other tradition, Mennonites encompass several understandings of the "believed" church, which functions as both a theological construct and an ideal. In their 1991 edited collection *Mennonite Peace Theology: A Panorama of Types*, John Richard Burkholder and Barbara Nelson Gingerich identify the ten types of peace theology and a host of related ecclesiologies.[1] Since the current discussion cannot cover all types of "believed" Mennonite church, I choose to analyze three Mennonite approaches – messianic community, missional church, and shalom church – to make the case that becoming a critical intercultural church is part of Mennonite ecclesiology. For the messianic community, John Howard Yoder is the representative author; for the missional church, Lois Barrett and Robert Suderman are the main voices; and for shalom church, Duane Friesen and Malinda Berry are the key theologians. I choose these approaches and representative authors for three reasons. First, these authors are authoritative leaders and scholars in their respective fields, and they have written extensively enough that I can engage critically with their scholarship. Second, while these approaches share some common ground, like their Anabaptist perspective, peace witness, and a mindset that aims to challenge Christendom, they are also distinct enough to be contrasted. The presence of various distinct approaches is crucial if we are to present a wide range of Mennonite ecclesiologies. Third, these three types become central ingredients in my proposals for the Mennonite Church to become intercultural. By presenting and analyzing these types, I hope to identify the wide range of theological ideals that Mennonites are already affirming, especially in their understanding of the church, world, mission, and difference. Laying out this work is important as it allows me to demonstrate the gap between the believed and the experienced church; it also serves to identify Mennonite theological resources that can empower the church to become a critical intercultural community in Canada.

In the pursuit of a contextualized Mennonite ecclesiology, it is noteworthy to recognize that John Howard Yoder and Lois Barrett were professors at the Anabaptist Mennonite Biblical Seminary (AMBS) in Elkhart, Indiana, and that Malinda Berry currently continues to teach there. Although situated in the United States, AMBS stands as a testament to the collaborative spirit between MC Canada and MC USA, evident in its binational status, diverse student body, and a board of directors that includes representatives from both countries. While the faculty at AMBS may not all be of Canadian origin, the majority of professors in the seminary engage in writing, teaching, and research that demonstrates a profound consideration of the Canadian context. Likewise, Duane Friesen maintains strong ties with Canadian Mennonites and has delved into the nuances of the Canadian context. This commitment is reflected in his 2000 book *Artists, Citizens, Philosophers: Seeking the Peace of the City*, which he penned while completing a residency in Canada.[2] Furthermore, even though Robert Suderman is a Canadian scholar and church leader, he has also engaged deeply with his US counterparts.

For each approach regarding the "believed" church, I first briefly identify core theological understandings that inform what it means to be a church. I then examine more specifically what each ecclesiology teaches about difference and diversity, both within the church and outside of it, with the aim of naming basic theological affirmations and practices that can lead churches toward becoming intercultural. Ultimately, intercultural engagement is about how to celebrate difference and how to interact respectfully and genuinely with people from diverse ethnocultural and racial backgrounds.

Messianic Community

Perhaps the most popular Mennonite ecclesiological perspective is that of the messianic community, with John Howard Yoder as its main representative. Although other Mennonite scholars like Wilbert Shenk, David Shenk, Larry Millar, and Neal Blough also write about messianic community, these authors primarily rely on Yoder's work. It is for this reason that I see Yoder as representative of this approach. However, it's vital to recognize the serious issues surrounding Yoder, including sexual and power abuse, which have stirred debates about the relevance of his theological contributions. Rachel Waltner Goossen's research into Yoder's misconduct, detailed in her 2015 article "'Defanging the Beast': Mennonite Responses to John Howard Yoder's Sexual Abuse," is pivotal.[3] Her study, initiated at the invitation of MC USA's Discernment Group, included consulting the archives of both the AMBS and MC USA. Goossen's work was critical in revealing the extent of Yoder's behaviour and the institutional responses it elicited, providing a deeper understanding of the impact and legacy of Yoder's actions within the Mennonite community and beyond.

Goossen shows how Yoder devised his own guidelines and selected individual women, referring to them as "sisters." His activities spanned a range of behavior, including different types of physical touch and sexual interactions. Yoder framed these actions as part of a continuum of theological and ethical exploration. His behaviour resulted in significant harm to many women, affecting their personal and professional lives. Despite an awareness of his actions, institutional responses were limited, focusing more on protecting Yoder's reputation and the AMBS's interests rather than addressing the harm caused to his victims.[4]

The theological community's reaction to Yoder's sexual abuse has been varied. Scholars like David Cramer, Jenny Howell, Paul Martens, Jonathan Tran, Denny Weaver, and Gerald Mast contend that Yoder's theological views remain useful and insightful, even in light of his personal failures to uphold these beliefs.[5] Conversely, scholars like Isaac Villegas, Lisa Schirch, Carolyn Holderread Heggen, Susan Brooks Thistlethwaite, Peter Dula, and Malinda Berry argue that his abuse is intertwined with his writings, warranting a cautious examination and use of his work. In this context, it is inappropriate to simply regard Yoder as having fallen short of his own beliefs.[6] Additionally, there are scholars, including Elizabeth Soto Albrecht, Nancy Bedford, and other feminist theologians who contributed to the book *Liberating the Politics of Jesus*, who entirely dismiss Yoder's work and instead draw from their own experiences and resources to construct Anabaptist-Mennonite theologies.[7] In pursuit of a project that critically assesses a wide spectrum of peace theologies and provides a theo-ethical perspective, I include Yoder's writings here not to endorse them or their author, but rather to critically assess their content and to offer a more inclusive, intercultural, and deeply rooted Mennonite theology. Whether or not theologians formally cite Yoder, his theological perspectives remain widely accepted and embedded in Mennonite theologies. Hence, rather than shying away from these theological views, it is crucial that we engage them directly in order to reconstruct for a more holistic understanding of Mennonite ecclesiologies.

One of the core beliefs of the messianic community approach is that the church has been called to actively engage in the world. As late as the 1960s, the understanding that the church should withdraw from society was predominant among Mennonites of European descent; this was primarily based on their understanding of nonconformity, and also on the biblical nonresistance perspective articulated by Harold Bender and Guy Hershberger in early 1940s.[8] During the 1960s, however, Yoder made strong and convincing arguments for why Mennonites needed to be more involved in the world through his books *The Christian Witness to the State* and *The Politics of Jesus*.[9] Moreover, he emphasized a particular way of engaging, following the example of Jesus. In other words, Yoder called on the church to interact in this world from a position of servanthood instead of a position of power and domination. He explains that many traditional churches during the Christendom period interacted in the world from the former position. Several present-day churches still pursue a modified form of this approach, by uncritically blessing and defending a specific political direction within society. In sum, through his writings, Yoder is not asking whether the church should be political or apolitical as much as advocating for churches to choose the right kinds of political engagement, following the example of Jesus.[10]

There is an intrinsic connection between Christology and ethics/discipleship in the ecclesiology of the messianic community. Yoder writes that through Jesus, this new "aeon" – this new creation or the new age of the kingdom of God – has arrived. Jesus showed and taught his disciples how to live as people of this new creation; therefore, anyone who is a follower of Jesus should follow in his steps. The people who live according to this new way of life are called the church or the messianic community. In this new aeon, Jesus is now the Lord of both the world and the church, which means that, rather than a bifurcated sense of ethics – one set of standards for the church and another for the world – there is just one. Yoder recognizes that the core difference between the world and the church is that the former does not recognize Jesus's lordship and therefore will not live according to his rule. Hence, he states, "Church and world are not two compartments under separate legislation or two institutions with contradictory assignments, but two levels of the pertinence of the same Lordship. The people of God are called to be today what the world is called to be ultimately."[11] To witness Jesus's lordship of the world, the church is called to be the royal priesthood. Instead of withdrawing from the world, the church has to be an "evangelical nonconformist," which means not conforming to the world, holding on to the teachings of Jesus, and engaging in the world and witnessing this new creation.[12] By stating this, Yoder is pushing against the historic "withdrawal" version of non-conformity in Mennonite theology.

To explain further how the messianic community should engage in the world, Yoder asserts that Jesus began his "original revolution" not by recruiting armed fighters, like the Zealots, or by starting a secluded spiritual group, like the Essenes, but by creating a distinct (messianic) community with its own set of values that deviated from the norms of Roman society, and with its own coherent way of living out the teachings of Jesus. This community constitutes a new humanity, a new society that one joins by voluntarily pledging allegiance to Jesus and committing to living in an inter-ethnic (in this case between Jews and Gentiles) community where people are mixed ethnically, racially, culturally, and economically. Instead of relating to each other based on existing worldly norms, according to which one seeks to dominate the other, the members of such a community would follow a new way of life and a new pattern of relationship between different groups. Yoder writes that Jesus taught these people new ways of "dealing with one another, with ethnic differences, with social hierarchy, with money, with offenses, with leaderships, and with power."[13] Therefore, the discipleship of the messianic community is paradigmatically bound to Jesus's way, practice, and ministry.

For Yoder, Christians genuinely practising, within a community, the new way of life that Jesus taught is related to witnessing and mission; the teachings and the new norm that the church received from Jesus are actually what Jesus requires for the larger society to live. Therefore, embodying the teachings becomes a concrete way of witnessing in front of the world how to live according to God's will. In his book *Body Politics*,

Yoder presents five early church practices that offer alternatives to the existing oppressive social and religious systems: binding and loosing, disciples breaking bread together, baptism and the new humanity, the fullness of Christ, and the rule of Paul.[14] *Binding and loosing* comes from a rabbinic term that implies forgiveness, moral/spiritual discernment, and reconciliation. Integrating this with his interpretation of Matthew 18:18 and John 20:23, Yoder explains that to bind and loose means to forgive (or, alternatively, to withhold forgiveness) and to make moral decisions mutually when there is a conflict or disagreement within one's community. *Breaking bread* is not simply a sacramental act and an abstract theological concept but an actual practice of sharing food and having fellowship with people from diverse ethnocultural backgrounds and socio-economic positions. This practice further invites believers to share economic resources with one another as an alternative way of living in society's unjust economic system. *Baptism* is an act of joining the body of Christ to the new humanity. Since we join this new inter-ethnic community where other barriers such as gender and class have also been broken down, a Christian task is to work for inter-ethnic reconciliation and harmony, in which we believe that we are created as equals and also truly treat others as equals. *The fullness of Christ* is a belief that God has given every member of the church gifts, and so everyone has an important role to play. Hence, "no role is more central than any other, and the least honored roles should be most affirmed."[15] This practice emphasizes the dignity and equality of each individual while preventing the concentration of power among a few leaders. Inspired by the apostle Paul's instructions in Acts 16 and 1 Corinthians 14, Yoder writes that *the rule of Paul* shows us how to hold a meeting so that everyone has an opportunity to share. It entails un-coerced consensus and dialogue that seeks to find truth mutually and "listening to the Spirit speaking through each other."[16] All of these are practices for the new peoplehood to follow; Yoder then shows how they can be extended and applied to the larger society.

From this brief analysis of the messianic community, several insights emerge that have ecclesiological implications for difference and diversity. As Jesus taught non-violence, in any relationship and even in the way we communicate, Christians should renounce any kind of violence when engaging with difference, including physical, verbal, and even structural abuse and harm. Non-violent witness and relationship can only occur when Christians surrender the desire to shape society through domination and manipulation.[17] Indeed, as Christians give up their desire to dominate and control, they need to respect the dignity of each person in the fullest sense: physical, spiritual, emotional, psychological, cultural, and so on. Furthermore, drawing on Jesus's example of servanthood, we should relate to one another with humility, meaning that we must always be open to the other, recognizing that we do not have all the answers and that we might be wrong. This approach calls for what John Roth describes as "epistemological humility,"[18] and what Christian Early and Ted Grimsrud call a "nonviolence epistemology."[19] These five practices also instruct us to apply mutuality, equality, and particularly when engaging with difference, and to be more attentive to those who are "least honoured." This involves creating a more egalitarian power structure, fostering a culture of respect, and attending to the voices of marginalized people. Moreover, the practice of breaking bread invites the church to attend to the economic and material needs of others and to break down the barriers that divide people.

Yoder writes that Christians should not be concerned about the disagreements that result from diversity (or difference). He states that diversity is the original intent of God and that the presence of multiple cultures and languages therefore reveals God's will.[20] In a diverse place like the church, disagreement is natural. Thus, Yoder asserts, disagreement should not be a reason for division, but rather a call for reconciliation.[21] The goal of unity "is not that people agree and, therefore, work together but that where they disagree, they need to talk together with a view to reconciliation."[22]

From Yoder, Mennonites learn that in engaging with difference, people do not need to give up their cultural identities and practices. Drawing on the teaching of the apostle Paul in Ephesians 2, Yoder points out that in the new inter-ethnic community, Jews and Gentiles do not need to give up their respective cultural identities and their ways of knowing and being; he further argues that focusing on one group does not necessarily mean dismissing the other. Rather, in this new community, each group is meaningless without the other because each member has become the necessary condition for the existence of the other. Without being connected with and helping each other, these communities cannot live and thrive. In other words, the other has now become so meaningful and significant to each group that a real sense of community cannot exist without it. While maintaining cultural differences, each person can work mutually to build up the body of Christ, understanding that without others, the church cannot be complete. In sum, differences exist in the church, and these differences actually enrich and build up the church. Therefore, in Christ, unity should be strived for as each member respects and values those differences.

Yoder's passion for ecumenism and his insight on true conversation also provide insights on how to engage with difference. While Yoder identifies himself as a Mennonite scholar, he explains his "normative testimony is 'catholic.'"[23] In other words, what he writes is not only for Mennonites, but for all Christians. To work and to advance ecumenical dialogue is one of his main interests, and this is reflected in his understanding of the messianic community. Christians confess the lordship of Jesus, and so the one who binds them together is Jesus. Since all Christians have one Lord and one body, ecumenism or unity among Christian denominations is an essential aspect of the messianic community. Furthermore, dialoguing and working toward unity is also one of the missions of the church. In Yoder's words, the "unity of Christians is a *theological* imperative first of all in the sense that its reasons arise out of the basic truth commitments of the gospel and the church's intrinsic mission."[24]

Not only does Yoder underscore the importance of working for Christian unity, but he also explains what true conversation is and how it can be accomplished. According to him, past ecumenical dialogues were more like "information sharing" sessions: each denomination got to know more about and gain new insights from other denominations, but instead of leading to an agreement, such dialogues "crystalized fundamental differences," and therefore prevented further communication. Yoder argues that a true conversation is a dialogue in which "there is movement toward agreement, motivated by appeal to an authority recognized by both parties."[25] Simply put, such conversation requires both parties to seek a mutually recognized authority; only then can both parties have recourse to "ultimate proof" along with the willingness to change positions when such proof has been marshalled. Since Christian unity is a theological reality made possible by Christ and a mission that all Christians should pursue, the question is whether we accept the Jesus revealed in scripture as the final authority. Yoder clarifies that this does not mean that all other theological and traditional sources should be condemned, or that we are required to interpret the Bible through an "infantile literalism"; rather, we should mutually abandon any particular theological source as a "canon of interpretation."[26] For him, all other sources should be below Christ and scripture. It is only when Christians recognize that Christ and the scriptures are the ultimate revelation that a true conversation can happen.

Since ecumenical unity is the nature of the church and its calling, all Christians are called to engage in this true conversation with fellow Christians across every border. This commitment should be taken so seriously that we are willing to give up other loyalties, such as patriotism, and we should demand the same commitment and obedience of other fellow Christians. Hence, to "accept less, to believe less, than that *this* is the unity that because it is a promise is a command as well, would be to deny the Lord."[27] Working toward a true conversation that leads to unity is the nature of the church, the mission of the church, and the work of Christian discipleship. Through this kind of conversation and unity, as Jesus said, the world will believe in him. The unity and the conversation that Yoder is arguing for is not simply a common denominator among different denominations or a false unity in which we tolerate others; rather, it is a mutual transformation whereby both parties learn to converse with one another with a view toward reconciliation.

Messianic community's approach to ecumenical dialogue and practical ways of working toward a true conversation can provide resources for healthy engagement with difference in several ways. Yoder encourages Christians to go beyond tolerance and the acceptance of a "common denominator," because these attitudes merely seek a minimum of interaction with other traditions, and do not reflect the authentic unity to which Jesus calls the churches. In a true conversation, all involved are mutually transformed. For followers of Jesus, this type of engagement is not optional – it is the very nature and mission of the church and an essential aspect of Christian discipleship. Not engaging with it is like denying Jesus.

Yoder is clearly aware that the divisions among Christians pertain not only to different Christian denominations. The real divisions, he states, "are between rich and poor, between liberal and conservative, between races, between east and west," and they exist in each congregation and each denomination.[28] Thus, differences exist not just outside of church tradition but also within the church; this further reinforces the call for each Christian to work for unity among. Rather than stemming from difference itself, division occurs as a result of marginalization, oppression, and exclusion. One of the concrete ways that Christians can engage with difference is to have true conversations in which we seek a genuine agreement based on the Jesus revealed in scripture.

Missional Church

The concept of a "missional church" has developed from the long-standing ecumenical effort to integrate missions and ecclesiology. Although this ecclesial perspective emerged out its own separate discourse, it also overlaps with several important aspects of the messianic community, like emphasizing the importance of discipleship, and noting that everyone, not only a few specialists, is called for missional work. The term "missional" emerged in the 1950s from the International Missionary Council's discussion of *missio Dei*, the mission of God. The emphasis "was on the mission as God's, not the church's, and on the church, participating in the *missio Dei*, as missionary by its very nature."[29] At a time when missions were considered an evangelizing enterprise to spread the gospel into the non-Western world, early missional church thinkers in the 1950s saw the necessity of re-evangelizing modern Western society. As a result, the seminal edited volume *Missional Church: A Vision for the Sending of the Church in North America* was published in 1988 after a rich conversation among theologians, scholars, and missionaries on the topic of culture, the gospel, and the church in the North American context, meaning Canada and the United States. Observing the shifting reality in Northern America,[30] the authors of this book made six essential arguments: (1) the church in Northern America is now located within a dramatically changed context; (2) the good news announced by Jesus as the reign of God needs to shape the identity of the missional church; (3) the missional church with its identity rooted in the reign of God must live as an alternative community in the world; (4) the missional church needs to understand that the Holy Spirit cultivates communities that represent the reign of God; (5) the missional church is to be led by a missional leadership that focuses on equipping all of God's people for mission; and (6) the missional church needs to develop missional structures for shaping its life and ministry, in addition to practising missional connectedness within the larger church.[31]

Several Mennonite leaders embraced the *missional church* concept promoted by the book because they believed that it describes aptly Mennonite core convictions. A missional church encourages individual churches to engage actively in society, maintains a strong connection between ecclesiology and Christology, emphasizes the need to be an alternative community, and invites everyone to be participants in God's missional work (which reflects the belief of the priesthood of all believers, one of the central beliefs of the Mennonites).[32] According to distinguished Mennonite missiologist Wilbert Shenk, the Great Commission in the New Testament was one of the key beliefs of sixteenth-century Anabaptists, and Anabaptist laypeople fully participated in evangelization. As a result, he claims that being missional is part of Mennonites' "DNA."[33] Another reason why Mennonites, particularly MC USA, embraced the missional concept is because they saw it as offering "a usable future." Stanley Green, then executive director of the Mennonite Mission Network, explains that in the process of merging the General Conference Mennonite Church and the (Old) Mennonite Church, it seemed that the church was heading "in the direction of an embrace of a generic white North American identity accommodated to the impulse of Christendom."[34] To resist this, at the 2001 assembly, delegates unanimously consented to commit themselves to the "identity of becoming a missional people in the twenty-first century."[35] Being aligned with missional church discourse and wanting to push further the missional identity within the Mennonite circle, some influential Mennonite leaders and scholars, such as Lois Barrett and Robert Suderman, have incorporated this discourse within Mennonite ecclesiology.

In this book, I mostly examine the missional church discourse within the Mennonite circle, since this project focuses on Mennonite ecclesiology. In analyzing the missional church, I draw particularly on the work of Lois Barrett and Robert Suderman because I see them as authoritative scholars and leaders in this ecclesiology within the Mennonite circle. Lois Barrett is not only a respected Mennonite scholar but is also one of the few theologians who writes about the missional church from an Anabaptist perspective. She taught at AMBS and also was a long-time denominational leader in the General Conference. Robert Suderman has a PhD in New Testament studies and taught for years in the Colombian Mennonite Seminary and continues to be guest teacher around the world. He became an influential voice when he served as general secretary of MC Canada and the secretary of the Mennonite World Conference Peace Commission. He is one of the prominent Mennonite leaders who actively advocates for Mennonite churches to become missional.

One of the fundamental theological perspectives of the missional church is that the church exists not to serve itself but rather to participate in God's mission of reconciliation. Barrett writes that during Christendom (fourth to eighteenth century),[36] when everyone within a Christian nation was considered to be Christian, mission involved missionaries going to non-Christian territories. However, as Christendom died out, churches were no longer at the centre of society. For this reason, where we are currently living can also be considered a mission field. The missional church identifies as one that is "being sent" – as opposed to a "sending" church – meaning that the church as a whole participates in God's mission and in the work that God has already been doing. The church is invited to be part of this work rather than focusing on itself as the locus of expansion or the key dynamic figure. Its being "called out" and sent into the world to serve is a central part of its identity, rather than merely sending an aspect of itself overseas. Hence, all the activities of the church are seen through the lens of mission; activities like outreach, congregational life, and church rituals are efforts to embody God's mission.[37]

Before exploring more specifically how the missional church bears witness to the world, Barrett explains that all human beings live in and among a culture or group of cultures, and this is true of the church as well. She points out that the gospel is expressed within a culture. There is no such thing as a cultureless gospel; it is shaped by and interpreted through one's culture. Therefore, the gospel is always "communicated with the thought constructs and practices prevalent within the cultural setting of the church in a specific time and place."[38] And yet, the gospel also leads beyond one's cultural thought forms and customs to the distinctive culture of the kingdom of God proclaimed by Jesus. Some particular traits of this distinctive culture involve offering one's primary allegiance to Jesus, living out the vision of the reign of God through economic justice and Jubilee, practising mutual aid, using power in non-violent ways, and concretely living out the Sermon on the Mount.[39] As a result, the church is always bicultural and bilingual. The church has to continually translate the gospel in a way that the surrounding culture can understand and, at the same time, help the believers in that culture to move more toward living according to the lifestyle and communal identity of God's people.

According to Barrett, this type of relational dynamic is referred to as "nonconforming engagement," in contrast to "isolated nonconformity" and "co-opted engagement."[40] The church lives within the surrounding culture but is not controlled by it. When it engages, it critiques values and norms that oppose the distinctive culture of the kingdom of God, but it also affirms those aspects of culture that do not contradict the kingdom of God. As a missional church, this interaction is not optional; the theological reality is that the church is "sent out" on behalf of the reign of God, and so a church cannot be insulated. As Barrett explains, when the church engages the world, in order to be truly apostolic, it must not participate in a Christendom mindset, an attitude whereby the church primarily seeks to support the status quo instead of being prophetic and missional.[41] Hence, in this encounter, "the church may sometimes *be affirming* of that culture ... [may] sometimes *be* nonconforming ... [and] may sometimes *propose* to parts of society or government actions that move it closer to Jesus' way ... The church will always seek to *demonstrate* the Jesus way, to be a sign of God's future."[42]

Another proponent of the missional church, Robert Suderman, invites fellow Mennonites to reinterpret Mennonite theology and practices through a missional lens in his book *Re-imagining the Church*. Suderman connects God's reconciling mission with hospitality and discipleship. He asserts that if God's mission is to bring together individuals from every nation and tribe to create a people to share God's purposes in the world, then the Christian's mission is not only preaching God's message but also practising hospitality and embracing everyone. Christians should be "wildly inclusive" of all people. This practice is related to discipleship because it requires radical obedience.[43]

Moreover, through the missional church lens, Suderman encourages North American Mennonite churches to be part of a global communion and to collaborate with churches around the world. Since all contexts are in need of the gospel message of Jesus, and not only the Global South, through global communion, local churches in Northern America need to hear and learn how God is working in different parts of the world. And through this communion, seek mutual partnership and transformation.[44]

The missional church concept can also empower us to engage with difference. Christians are sent into the world to be part of God's reconciling work; as a result, engagement with difference is inevitable. As we interact with people from other societies and cultures, in light of the teachings of Jesus, we need to be aware of how these people (through various values, norms, and ideologies) form and malform our identities, perception of others, and our way of dialogue, and then work together toward God's will. We can start by celebrating the goodness in each culture (without "essentializing" any) before critiquing aspects that oppress people and stand against the gospel of Jesus, and later working for transformation.

In working toward reconciliation with difference, the church is called to be "wildly inclusive" and to embrace the other because it is part of radical discipleship. Christians are discouraged from perceiving the other through the lens of the dominant culture, and instead are enjoined to view them through God's eyes and to welcome them. This can be done by learning and embodying countercultural practices, habits, and liturgies that encourage hospitality. Believers should not conform to the norms and the values of the dominant culture; rather, they should conform to God's will and break down barriers that divide God's people. In practising hospitality, Christians become intentionally mindful that we are part of the global church, and accordingly, seek to be in communion with churches around the world, including people from diverse ethnocultural and racial backgrounds. It is through this global communion that our understanding of God will be broadened and deepened, thereby opening possibilities for mutual transformation.

Shalom Church

The third Mennonite approach that I examine here is the shalom church, and for articulating the character of this approach, I choose Duane Friesen and Malinda Berry as primary spokespersons. Duane Friesen is a theologian and professor emeritus at Bethel College, and shalom is one of the key components of his ecclesiology. Malinda Berry, who is associate professor of theology and ethics at AMBS, is included here not only because shalom is a central factor in her theology, but also because she labels her theology as "shalom political theology." Certainly, most Mennonite theologians write about peace, but both Friesen and Berry intentionally use the term "shalom" because it reflects a much broader understanding of peace.

To understand how the shalom church differs from the messianic community, before analyzing the view of these two representatives, it is important to know how they situate themselves in the spectrum of Mennonite understandings of discipleship. In the 1940s and '50s, H.S. Bender and G.F. Hershberger advocated for non-political discipleship, and their view was widely accepted. A younger scholar, John Howard Yoder, began to advocate in his writings for a more active engagement on the part of the church in the world, especially by witnessing to the state – yet only within the framework of discipleship. He argues that Christians are "responsible" not for changing the world but for following the way of Jesus; transforming the world is God's problem. Yoder believes that by seeking to be "responsible" for worldly transformation, Christians will compromise their faith and belief. In contrast to the views put forth by Bender, Hershberger, and Yoder, both Lawrence Burkholder and Gordon Kaufman explicitly promoted the church's social responsibility. Burkholder writes that Mennonites are part of society, whether they reside in rural or urban locations, because they are already interconnected with surrounding communities and live within the economic systems and social structures of their given countries. For this reason, as a church and as individuals, Mennonites should be involved in the human struggle for justice and in the realms of economics and politics.[45] Kaufman also advocates for a more active political and social engagement, asserting that faithful living entails being involved in society and acting with social responsibility, because the love that the Bible teaches works actively and redemptively in an unjust society. Consequently, a withdrawal from society is akin to a failure to love, which compromises Christians' faith.[46] In between "sectarian ethics" and "social responsibility," Duane Friesen represents a middle ground (indeed, Yoder and Kaufman were both his teachers and influenced his theological orientation).[47] Malinda Berry's theological orientation largely aligns with Friesen's, although she brings new insights.

A crucial theological aspect of the shalom church approach is that it seeks to balance our ideal view of the church with a realistic understanding of human society, because shalom encompasses human reality. In *Artists, Citizens, and Philosophers*, Friesen proposes a church model for the Northern American context whose two main characteristics are "repentance" and "balanced realism." Friesen describes the church as a "treasure in clay jars," an expression he borrows from 2 Corinthians 4:7. The treasure (the church) has certain limitations because it is contained in the clay jars of imperfect human institutions; consequently, churches fail to live up to their ideals, and they disappoint people. Hence, he argues that when Christians talk about the role of the church, they should start with repentance – for the wrongs that the church has done to others and to its own members. He explains the crucial need for balanced realism, or a balance between our ideal (or "believed") view of the church and a realistic understanding of how human institutions work (the "experienced" church) in our given time and context.[48]

In order for the church to maintain this "balanced realism," Friesen asserts that it should strive to manage four critical tensions. The first is between the dignity, value, and gifts each individual has to offer and the importance of belonging to the body of Christ. Friesen is concerned that too much individualism or too much collectivism can be problematic.[49] The second is between the need for clear boundaries defining the identity of a community and the necessity of welcoming people from different cultural, religious, and socio-economic backgrounds. The third is between a clear sense of one's faith identity and vision and recognizing that one is also situated in a specific cultural and geographical context. Christians already share much with the larger culture around them, meaning that the boundary separating Christian and non-Christian is fairly fluid and difficult to distinguish. Friesen states that the church is not separate from society, that Christians are already in the world, and so they need to acknowledge this while maintaining a clear sense of their identity and vision. The fourth and final tension is between *being* the church and *doing* the work of mission in the larger society. Friesen draws on two contrasting ecclesiological perspectives here: The first is represented by people like Stanley Hauerwas and William Willimon, who argue that a church's primary task is to live according to its own story-formed way of life – *being* the church in contrast with the world. The second is represented by scholars like Ernst Troeltsch and H.R. Niebuhr, who state that Christians should move beyond the church and become politically involved with the larger society. Friesen argues for a balance between these two perspectives. This is a position he ascribes to scholars like Larry Rasmussen and Yoder. Yet, unlike Yoder, Friesen advocates for the church to assume an active social responsibility, an involvement in society that goes beyond the framework of discipleship. Friesen also emphasizes the importance of mission by stating that "the church is not genuinely the church without mission."[50] After offering a church model, Friesen suggests a list of "focal practices" that are faithful to Christ and that work to form one's moral character. The practices that he suggests focus on both being the church and doing the work of mission in the larger society.[51]

Another crucial aspect of the shalom church as an ecclesial approach is its conception of the church's active engagement in broader society. In *At Peace and Unafraid*, Friesen asserts that being Christian means to seek the kingdom of God, which is to work toward just relationships in one's personal interactions, in the larger society, and with God. This means one's responsibility is to develop a "gospel order," an order that provides "good news for the poor and liberty to the captives."[52] It is to transform our unjust and violent society into a just and peaceful one in which even marginalized people can flourish. Friesen connects the kingdom of God with a biblical vision of shalom. This vision is not simply an absence of war and violence, but one in which righteousness and social justice prevail, and in which everyone's basic necessities of life and well-being are secured. Since both of these visions, the kingdom of God and shalom, invite Christians to actively shape and transform the wider society through involvement in government and non-Christian organizations, Christians need to speak a language that non-Christians can understand. Thus, Friesen argues for Christians to be metaphorically multilingual.

The first step in this direction is for Christians to know their own "language" – the narrative that shapes their Christian identity and core convictions. Once this has been formed, Christians are ready and indeed called to go beyond their faith community and interact with non-Christians in public. While some Christians contend that relating with non-Christians requires them to abandon their Christian convictions and accept a "neutral" and secular discourse, Friesen argues that believers should bring their own faith traditions to this public dialogue instead of diluting them, engaging with the conviction that they are called to participate in the world where God has already been working. Christians should, however, reflect carefully on the appropriate way of engaging at a particular place and time and in the various contexts of their lives. For this to be done, wisdom is needed, which is comprised of a "blend of theological conviction with reason, experience, and an empirical understanding of how the world works."[53]

In arguing that Christians need to be multilingual, Friesen asserts that, beyond the language Christians use within the church, they ought to know at least four other "languages": those of prophetic witness, Christian vocation, the common good in democratic discourse, and middle axioms. Prophetic witness means confronting the powers and naming and unmasking evils that exist in our society. Christian vocation means that Christians need to be involved in different professional worlds. The common good in democratic discourse entails Christians contributing to the social goods that protect the lives and dignity of people. Friesen remarks that in this discourse, the virtues of democratic speech are required because Christians can otherwise try to dominate the conversation without actively listening. Christians can contribute to this common good by creating policies and shaping social structures that protect and cherish all people. Lastly, there is the concept of middle axioms, which Friesen borrows from Yoder, and Yoder from J.H. Oldham.[54] Middle axioms are ethical principles that are not specifically Christian but that nonetheless resonate with Christian faith and can be utilized as "bridges" between Christians and non-Christians. They call for people to live up to their own moral principles and ideals. Any group, organization, or state has its own moral principles and ideals; these might be different from those professed by Christians. While Christians cannot ask non-believers to follow Christian principles, Christians can at least ask non-believers to live up to their own ideals.

In sum, as a proponent of the shalom church, Friesen stresses the importance of finding a balance between various tensions that exist in our understanding of the church: striving to live according to our ideal view of the church while embracing a realistic understanding of human reality and society; rooting our church identity in our faith traditions and narratives while welcoming people from diverse ethnocultural, religious, and socio-economic backgrounds; having a clear identity and vision as a Christian while recognizing that one has multiple and intersectional identities; and focusing on both the *being* and the *doing* of the church. By balancing these tensions in a healthy manner, Mennonite churches can participate in the work of shalom. Since this work extends to the larger society, Friesen calls for Christians to be multilingual and to engage actively and aptly with non-Christians. Compared to this treatment of the messianic community and the missional church, Friesen places much more emphasis on the worldly aspects of human society – on human fragility, sin, and how people interact with one another through social structures. Moreover, he calls for the church to take a much more active involvement in society than that prescribed by Yoder's discipleship approach or the missional approach advocated by Barrett and Suderman.

Another proponent of the shalom church is Malinda Berry, who agrees that the church should maintain a balance between an ideal view of itself and a realistic understanding of human reality and society. Hence, she proposes a "shalom political theology" (SPT) from a feminist perspective that integrates Reinhold Niebuhr's theological anthropology, Martin Luther King Jr's perception of non-violence, and Doris Janzen Longacre's concept of nonconformity. She explains that these theologians provide tools to develop a multivalent outer and inner awareness of Christian life, by which they mean the group dynamic of a church, its institutional and interpersonal challenges, and how these relations are all connected to the rest of the world. Berry clarifies that this theological perspective is based less on a biblical or systematic theology in the classic, disciplinary sense of the term than on an integration of biblical study, theological reflection, and ethical engagement that seriously considers non-violence and nonconformity.[55]

Berry observes that the weaknesses of the messianic community's theology relate to its incapacity to help contemporary Mennonites make theological sense of current social problems and, further, to discern the sin and violence existing within the church community. These weaknesses then prevent solidarity with the oppressed and a striving toward social justice with marginalized people, as this theology does not address the present-day issues within and outside the church, such as clergy sexual abuse in the Roman Catholic Church, the HIV/AIDS crisis in the Black church, and others.[56] Therefore, Berry's approach is more "realistic" because it closely examines the sinfulness of the community of faith and human society. As it is for Friesen, a biblical vision of shalom is important for Berry; but she perceives it as connected to the vision of the kingdom of God preached by Jesus. This shalom has four dimensions: (1) economic and material well-being; (2) right relations between neighbours and nations, where there is no suffering and oppression; (3) moral and ethical dimensions of believers' lives, where Christians act in integrity and in truth; and (4) God's creation of peace between people and God, which results in the transformation of relationships with other people. As a result, as churches engage in the world, they need to consider all these dimensions if they seek holistic shalom. At the same time, they also need to recognize how sin (unbelief, rebellion, inordinate self-love, and self-deception) destroys relationships and how grace (forgiveness, repentance, humility, and renewed trust) works to preserve them. Only after Christians are aware of how both sin and grace exist and work in the church and world will they be prepared to understand how to strive toward shalom.[57]

Berry explains that she practices SPT in three concrete ways, drawn from the three theo-ethicists Niebuhr, King, and Longacre. The first is to name the influential people of a faith community. By doing this, we can see the power dynamic of a church and comprehend how things get worked out. This practice helps us speak more truthfully about the internal politics of a church. The second is to practise non-violent communication, in which one is committed to non-violence and seeks to communicate one's emotions and needs in a constructive way. Third, we must practise the circle process through which all voices are heard and valued. Berry practises this in all group involvements. She argues that SPT takes sin and power dynamics seriously because it is also about transforming human lives and relationships. If shalom focuses only on the spiritual and not on the entirety of human life – bodies, societies, relationships, power dynamics, the power of sin, culture, and historical existence – it becomes merely an abstract theological concept or ideology. A concrete and realistic understanding and practise of peace is necessary because a simplistic understanding disempowers Christians from engaging with the issues that arise in our church communities and society. It can also lead to a limited discipleship that does not fully encompass humans' relationship dynamics and social lives. For example, in a peace church, church members may treat each other individually with respect and non-violence while at the same time failing to recognize how certain policies and systems withing the church can lead to oppression and exclusion.

What does this "believed" shalom church approach teach about difference and diversity? Friesen's model of the church and the need to be multilingual help us to imagine a more robust engagement with difference. His model begins with repentance, the acknowledgment of one's past sins and personal limitations, and the willingness and commitment to mend one's broken relationships. This humble starting place is quite appropriate in the Northern American context, where the church is explicitly and implicitly involved in exclusionary and oppressive practices, such as supporting colonialism, racism, and ethnocentrism. Also, this model helps Christians to understand the limitations of human institutions. Such institutions are established by people in a certain time and for certain purposes, and they are maintained by those selected to wield power. Consequently, they are inevitability rigid and fixed, and they function under a hierarchical structure. These characteristics might keep them running, but they can exclude certain people, especially those who are at the margins. Without carefully noting that churches, as human institutions, are led by people, it is quite easy to be disappointed when we fail to live according to our ideals. When Christians engage with difference, we need to begin with self-examination, humbly inquiring into what harm we may have done and that requires repentance. Also, when Christians interact, we must be aware of how human institutions can present barriers and/or bridges.

Friesen's model also emphasizes the importance of striking a balance between welcoming outsiders and holding on to one's identity, which is a helpful idea in relationship to difference and diversity. Friesen sees the danger of accepting everything (which can lead to acquiescing to injustice), on the one hand, and holding rigidly to one's identity (which may exclude others), on the other. When engaging difference, an excessive preoccupation with identity can become exclusionary and unwelcoming. Additionally, having an awareness of the multiple, intersecting identities we each have is helpful. Being Christian does not mean that we have exclusively Christian identities, since we are also a part of the larger society. Each of us surely has many similarities with people whom we might consider "other."

As Christians continually working for a true conversation, we sometimes need to acknowledge that there are certain gaps that cannot be closed – and so we turn to middle axioms. For example, in the dialogue between Mennonite and Roman Catholic faiths, both agree on some points of convergence. However, although both Mennonites and Roman Catholics see the importance of peace and non-violence, the Catholic magisterium still upholds the just war theory and the use of violence for exceptional cases.[58] Both parties will continue to engage in dialogue; in the meantime, Mennonites can encourage Roman Catholics to live up to their own moral principles and ideals, and vice versa.

Building on Friesen's insights and adding important elements of her own, Berry invites the church to recognize and change its existing power dynamics. In striving for a constructive relationship, SPT leads Christians to engage in non-violent communication and a circle process in which everyone's voice can be heard, especially people who have been traditionally marginalized. Since SPT also concerns one's relationship with the wider society outside of the church, we may apply this analysis of power dynamics and this constructive engagement to a wide variety of societal contexts.

In this chapter, I juxtaposed three Mennonite approaches to the "believed" church to present a survey of theological ideals and practices that Mennonites are already affirming and claiming. From the three approaches identified here, one can discern a shared invitation for Mennonites to become more actively involved in the world. In contrast to the traditional view that the church needs to withdraw from society, the messianic community asserts an evangelical nonconformist approach, the missional church encourages a nonconformed engagement, and the shalom church advocates for both the missional work of the church and social responsibility. Building on internal ideals within each approach, I examined what each "believed" church teaches about difference and diversity within and outside of the church, and I demonstrated that these approaches (a) draw on Mennonite ideals in Northern America; (b) are open to difference and take the call to embrace difference seriously;

(c) engage with the power dynamics that exist within and between different communities; and (d) offer specific practices on how to engage well with difference. Hence, I use these three approaches as the primary resources to aspire and guide Mennonite churches in Canada to become intercultural.

Ecclesiology includes theological and sociological fields, the first naming the one, holy, catholic, and apostolic church (which is theological, established by Christ), and the second naming the visible, institutional, experienced church, which is fallible and ministered by people. Certainly, because they portray our aspired realities, theological ideals always outpace the historical, sociological, and empirical church experienced by people. To narrow the gap between the "believed" and the "experienced" church, it is important to examine the reality of the latter. By understanding the situated reality, we may analyze the prospects for realizing the "believed" church, aspiring to lessen the gap between that and the "believed" church, and to live out our fallible and limited versions of the church (a "realized eschatology"). For this reason, I now turn to the "experienced" church of the Mennonites in Canada and the effort to achieve full interculturality.

2

Experienced Church: The Church as a Sociological Reality

This chapter takes a closer look at the "experienced" church of Mennonite Church Canada. I aim neither to be comprehensive nor to get into specific details, which, while nonetheless wishing to honour each tradition in the complex landscape of Mennonite history in Canada, would be too large a task for this project. Instead, I document several key moments of change in which Mennonite identity has been revisited and boundaries renegotiated. This provides the necessary backdrop for the following chapters' analysis. Moreover, it provides resources for critical commentary in light of the "believed" church ideals, ways of living that act as guiding principles and toward which the church aspires. I explain these key moments of change first by providing a broad-stroke narrative of Mennonite history in Canada, specifically highlighting Mennonites who are part of MC Canada, while also covering other noteworthy features; and second by interpreting this history with reference to the sociological analysis offered by Mennonite historians and sociologists.

For this project, following the example of various Mennonite scholars and thinkers, my approach analyzes the "sacred canopy" of Mennonite peoplehood and how it has changed throughout Mennonites' presence in this land. Some Mennonite historians and sociologists utilize this "sacred canopy" concept – a term coined by Peter Berger – to understand who the Mennonites are and how their identities and ways of living have been negotiated and renegotiated. Leo Driedger, a Canadian Mennonite sociologist, was probably the first Mennonite scholar to incorporate it in analysis of the Mennonites, particularly in his book *Mennonite Identity in Conflict*. Together with Howard Kauffman, another Mennonite sociologist, Driedger uses this approach to comprehend modern Mennonites of European ancestry in their book *The Mennonite Mosaic*. Subsequently, observing how the Mennonite way of engaging with the world has changed throughout history, Driedger and Donald Kraybill applied this approach in *Mennonite Peacemaking*.[1] Berger asserts that, in order to protect their core values and ideologies, religious groups have what is called a "sacred canopy": as a tent canopy protects one from outside threats and requires several stakes to uphold it, religious communities create a "canopy," held up by several principal "stakes," to protect their religious convictions and cultures. And just as a canopy is mobile, so, too, can the sacred canopy be transferred to a new place. If certain stakes do not work any longer, they can be reinvested with new meanings, so that they continually protect the core identities and cultures from outer threats and meaninglessness.[2]

For the Mennonites, the concept of peoplehood functions as just such a "sacred canopy." Several Mennonite scholars have used the term "peoplehood" to portray the Mennonite community because they recognize that it is more than just a religious group. The late Calvin Redekop, an emeritus professor of sociology at Conrad Grebel University College, explains that to categorize the Mennonite community as a purely cultural/national or religious group does violence to its other aspects and characteristics; and so it is more accurate to describe it is as a peoplehood.[3] He describes Mennonite peoplehood as follows: "United by the religious faith cohering in the religious community, a community which has a unique cast and which provides a 'boundary' mechanism for identity. This identity forms the basis for a social bond which elaborates into family, neighborhood, and community systems. The interaction with the environment, however, constantly limits, changes, and directs the development of all aspects of the society."[4]

As Redekop asserts, Mennonite peoplehood is a social group with certain religious, cultural, ethnic, and communal aspects, even as the "boundary" of the peoplehood shifts. These various aspects are integrated into the understanding of peoplehood, but the religious aspect is the predominant identifier for the majority of Mennonites. As Frank Epp, a Canadian Mennonite historian, explains, although a long history of persecution caused the people to withdraw from society and utilize particular characteristics of peoplehood as barriers to outsiders, some religious aspects continuously encourage the Mennonites' "boundary" to be more porous and inclusive. He clarifies that he is not arguing for easily

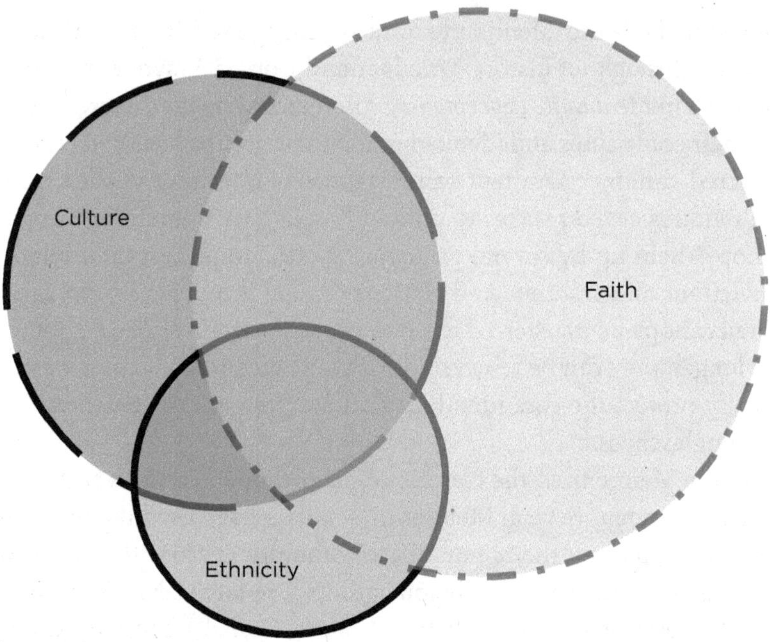

Figure 2.1 | Venn diagram illustrating the concept of Mennonite peoplehood as an intersection of culture, faith, and ethnicity, with each circle representing a component that contributes to the collective identity.

including anyone and everybody, but he understands the true peoplehood of God as having the heart of "the all-encompassing love of God in Christ for all of [God's] children."[5] He also reminds the Mennonites that Mennonite peoplehood exists for the sake of God's service and mission.

The Venn diagram pictured in figure 2.1 offers a visual representation of Mennonite peoplehood described by Redekop and Epp.

As you can see, faith is the largest identity factor, and the boundary around it is porous enough that anyone who commits to the Mennonite faith is welcomed. At the same time, there is the Mennonite culture, which is shaped and informed by Mennonite faith and ethnicity. Based on the cultural factor, Mennonites build community, establish institutions, create systems and policies, and form ways of life. While non-Mennonites can learn, enter, and benefit from the Mennonites' culture, community, and systems, one cannot easily claim that one is culturally Mennonite. Then, there is the ethnic aspect, which is to say those members with

Russian, Swiss, German, or Dutch backgrounds. Even though this factor is the smallest, it is still a significant component of Mennonite identity. This is the circle that is impermeable to outsiders, even to those who are married to ethnic Mennonites, and it is precisely this factor that impedes non-ethnic Mennonites from experiencing full belonging in the Mennonite Church.

The dynamic between these circles will be explained in further detail in chapter 3, but for now, I will explore three particular themes in this sacred canopy called Mennonite peoplehood: (1) how Mennonites' understanding of nonconformity (which is one of their core praxes and values) has changed; (2) how the church's engagement with the world has shifted; and (3) how diversity and difference have been dealt with in the Mennonite canopy. A broad survey of Mennonite history in Canada first provides the necessary context.

In the history of Canadian Mennonites, there have been several waves of migration. The first happened between 1785 and 1825, when Mennonites from Pennsylvania came to Canada to live under British rule and to search for new farmland. They are called "Swiss Mennonites," in reference to their Swiss ancestry. During this period, approximately 2,000 of these Mennonites settled in Ontario.[6] The next wave occurred between 1874 and 1880, when approximately 8,000 Russian Mennonites settled in Manitoba, through the help of the Swiss Mennonites. They migrated from Russia mainly because Mennonites were no longer exempted from military service in that country, and because they were no longer granted control over their education. Mennonites came to Canada by choice from the 1870s to the 1920s, but after that point they came as refugees, as did many after the Second World War. In 1919, after the Russian Revolution, Russian Mennonites moved to Canada with the assistance of the Mennonites who were already here. Around 22,000 of them migrated between 1922 and 1930, when the Soviet government prohibited people from emigrating. Another major wave of migration happened during the Second World War, when approximately 7,000 Russian Mennonites moved to Canada.

While there were waves of migration from the United States and Europe to Canada, Mennonites who already lived here also emigrated to other countries, like Mexico and Paraguay, because they no longer enjoyed autonomy in matters of education.[7] Around 7,700 Canadian Mennonites emigrated to these countries from 1922 to 1926, but later, in the 1950s, many returned to Canada – around 50,000 to Ontario alone.[8] Mennonite migration also occurred inside of Canada, as Mennonites moved within and between provinces. According to the Canadian census record of 2001, 191,000 Mennonites lived in Canada, and more than half of them in cities.[9]

From the earliest Mennonite settlement to the present day, drastic changes, both global and national, have forced Mennonites in Canada to shift their understanding of peoplehood. According to Canadian Mennonite historian T.D. Regehr, national factors like urbanization, modernization, the rise in economic prosperity, enforced public school education, the establishment of the universal Canada Pension Plan, and the influence of Christian fundamentalism deeply influenced the Mennonites. At the same time, international factors such as the world wars, global poverty, famine, civil wars in different countries, and global missions from ecumenical bodies also shifted how they engaged with the world.[10] As Mennonites experienced these changes, they knew that they could no longer simply "transfer" their sacred canopy, their understanding of peoplehood, to these new social realities. To keep their core convictions, they had no option but to "transform" their peoplehood. In the following section, I analyze further how they became a transformed people in these new social realities.

Nonconformity

Nonconformity has been one of the central beliefs of the Mennonites from the very beginning. Rather than following the norms and standards of the surrounding society, they believed that they needed to faithfully live out the teachings from the Bible, especially Jesus's teachings. This was and is a crucial part of the "believed" church. When the early Mennonites arrived in North America as a persecuted people, they continued using their German language and intentionally lived in rural, agricultural settings because of their belief in nonconformity. This belief and practice were tolerated and even fostered by general social conditions, including "the rural existence, the compact communities, the frontier psychology, and the spirit of individualism" that reigned among Mennonites.[11] But this "believed" church eventually underwent changes as the "experienced" church challenged members to be more relevant and to speak to the social changes they encountered.

As modernity developed and technology advanced, Mennonites moved to urban areas to work and live. In such contexts, geographical and social separation became almost impossible, with the result that maintaining nonconformity was no longer a simple matter. Up to this point, nonconformity had meant dressing differently, abstaining from worldly amusements, not having life insurance, not joining labour unions, and not being slothful. Confronted with drastic social change, Mennonites found themselves constantly interpreting and reinterpreting how they might practise nonconformity in a rapidly changing world, and how to embody their "believed" church in a different way. It is not surprising, then, that differing interpretations of nonconformity arose. Regehr asserts that

> Mennonite groups that had tried for centuries to separate themselves as much as possible from the outside world tended to be particularly suspicious of all technological, cultural, social, and political change. But even those most strongly committed to preservation of old ways could not avoid all change, and there were often sharp disagreements when some deemed it necessary, beneficial, or simply harmless to accept a particular innovation while others remained convinced that even small changes would lead to loss of essential aspects of their Christian life-style. Such disagreements resulted in much tension, and sometimes in fragmentation and schisms, particularly among the most traditional groups.[12]

In these disagreements, different groups applied nonconformity in diverse ways. Epp explains that at least five distinct forms of nonconformity or separation were articulated in the 1930s: geographical, institutional, ethical, cultural/national, and chronological (or dispensational) separation.[13] Geographical separation occurred via efforts to locate in rural settings so that the people would be less influenced by the surrounding society. Institutional separation was done by establishing institutions and organizations and encouraging Mennonites to primarily remain in these institutions throughout their different stages of life. For example, children and youth would go to Mennonite schools, adults would have their bank accounts in Mennonite credit unions, people would hire or be hired by other Mennonite professionals, and so on. Even though the Mennonites would be in an urban setting, by organizing their lives around different Mennonite institutions, they would live a separate lifestyle.

Ethical separation was lived out by being actively involved in society, in such areas as economics and civics, but instead of giving loyalty to the country and the political leaders, Mennonites would seek God's will and make every effort to live out Anabaptist-Mennonite core values. Cultural/national separation occurred among certain Mennonite communities in Canada because some were loyal to German culture; some of these even admired Adolf Hitler. Thus, most Mennonites made an effort to differentiate themselves from their pro-German brethren. Lastly, there were Mennonites who sought chronological separation, meaning dispensationalist fundamentalism. They focused mostly on saving souls, converting Jews, and advocating for the strict the separation of earthly and political realms. Epp clarifies that these distinct forms of nonconformity were modified, with a single group often displaying a combination of these and other forms. The majority of Mennonite churches that are part of MC Canada have embraced ethical separation. They are aware that geographical isolation is no longer possible, and so, rather than separating themselves from Canadian society, they have chosen to be part of it while living out an alternative value system and way of life, although many continue to work closely with Mennonite institutes.

Epp describes the particular version of nonconformity that the majority of members of General Conference Mennonite Church and Mennonite Church congregations in Canada have embraced as "accommodating" to social change. He differentiates here between the notions of accommodation and assimilation: for him, accommodation means adjusting to new social changes while holding on to one's identity, whereas assimilation means being absorbed, including one's identity, into the surrounding culture. Following this understanding, T.D. Regehr also uses the term "accommodation" to describe the majority of MC Canada. To him, the assimilated groups are Mennonites who became part of contemporary secular society as well as those who joined the evangelical stream of Christianity. By being Mennonites without religious identification or by embracing evangelicalism, they have lost their distinct Anabaptist-Mennonite identity and beliefs.[14] Another well-known Mennonite historian, Samuel Steiner, describes the majority stance as "assimilating," and the other groups as Separatist Conservatives, Evangelical Conservatives, and Old Orders.[15] While Steiner does not explain why he opted for the term "assimilation," his understanding of assimilation is clearly different from Epp's and Regehr's; the assimilated group that Steiner identifies has not given up their distinct Anabaptist-Mennonite identity and beliefs, even though their visible appearance and lifestyle might look similar to modern people, unlike the Old Order Mennonite groups. Whatever term one might use to explain the majority stance of MC Canada, historians agree that while the Mennonites have lost some of their distinct characteristics, they have maintained other traits, and also rediscovered "some that had been neglected in the rural enclaves but which were relevant to life in a modern Canadian setting."[16] These include missional engagement and offering relief and developmental services to those who are in need. To avoid confusion, I use the term "accommodation" to name the process of adaptation to new social changes in which these Mennonites hold on to their identities and beliefs while reinterpreting their communal identity and the "believed" church.

Even among the accommodating Mennonites, there was a wide range of "believed" church theological diversity regarding what nonconformity means and how it should be practised in Canadian society. Although this diversity triggered some divisions, it did not threaten overall unity. As those believing in ethical separation became more active in society and politics, they became more vocal about peacemaking by forming a Mennonite Central Committee office in Ottawa to lobby the government, and by supporting Christian Peacemaker Teams (now called Community Peacemaker Teams). They addressed several social and political issues, and some of them held high public office. Later on, they started to get the attention of the mass media and were acknowledged for their work ethic, relief work, refugee sponsorship programs, and disaster assistance. Without discarding nonconformity, MC Canada interpreted and reinterpreted this doctrine in the face of profound social change, ultimately arriving at a different understanding it. These endeavours of readjustment and accommodation provide substance to the claim that churches shifted as they "experienced" change, challenging and influencing the "believed" conception of the church to be much more relevant, well-defined, and contextualized, instead of getting rid of the belief in nonconformity altogether.

Diversity and Difference

As Mennonites experienced and accommodated themselves to various social changes, the community also became significantly more diverse in various senses, including racially and ethnically. Since historians and sociologists indicate that modernization is one of the main causes of contemporary social change, it is important to examine what modernization is and how it has affected Canadian Mennonites. Being aware that modernization, modernity, and the modern are slippery concepts, Leo Driedger and Donald Kraybill define modernization as the "massive changes, prodded by technology, that transform the social arrangements and collective consciousness of an entire society over time. The social conditions produced by modernization are commonly called modernity."[17] Modernization shaped the lives of all communities in North America, even the Mennonites, notwithstanding the fact that its effects were delayed in the Mennonite context due to the community's commitment to nonconformity. One key feature of modernity is pluralism in all areas of human social life – and this profoundly changed the Mennonite community.[18]

Driedger and Kraybill explain that until the early nineteenth century, Mennonites in North America were mostly rural people; by 1972, only 11 per cent were still farming, and the rest had gone to suburban and urban places to pursue a wide array of education and occupations. The authors note various consequences of these changes:

> Vacating the farm and entering new professions required higher education, which some 33 percent had obtained by 1972. Modern means of travel as well as the pursuit of higher education and professional jobs ruptured the bonds of stability in traditional Mennonite communities and splintered the plausibility structures that in earlier years had provided a supportive roost for nonresistance. The modernizing experience not only pulled Mennonites in from the fringes of society; it also propelled them upward in social

status. No longer a persecuted minority, many Mennonites in the twentieth century were enjoying upward social mobility.[19]

Accordingly, diverse perspectives and voices began to multiply and flourish within the Mennonite community.

The three main indicators of modernization in Mennonite communities were urbanization, education, and occupational status; all three affected how Mennonites interacted in the world.[20] Faced with greater exposure to society, Mennonites learned more diverse perspectives from their educational institutions, engaged in various professions and occupations, and became increasingly pluralistic as a community. This diversity changed not only the processes of ascertaining and maintaining unity in the midst of diversity, but also matters of mission work and witness. Through modernization, as Driedger and Kraybill point out, governments in Northern America focused on providing social welfare to the people in need. As a result, governments not only helped the Mennonites by offering federal aid to their institutes, like colleges and health centres, but also provided opportunities for Mennonites to be more involved in society through various civil services. Furthermore, collaboration between the government and the Mennonites meant that Mennonites could create and operate alternate service programs for conscientious objectors, granting capacity for nonconformity at a societal level. Democratic societies that embraced freedom of religion, accepted religious minorities, and respected conscientious objectors influenced Mennonites who previously had strong negative views of the state, inviting them to reconsider their understanding of the relationship between the state and the church. For example, Mennonites collaborated with the government to reduce poverty, and they created programs to welcome and accommodate refugees in Canada. Additionally, international conflicts like the Korean War, the Vietnam War, and the nuclear arms race forced Mennonites to reconsider how they should work with the state. All of these social factors challenged and invited Mennonites to find new ways of living in this new reality and engaging with governments and non-Mennonite organizations.

As Mennonites experienced social change, they also witnessed an increase in pluralistic views and beliefs within their communities. While pluralism does not always bring division, for the Mennonites, it triggered several schisms in the community. Redekop pinpoints six factors that caused schisms in the Mennonite community from the time of its first presence in Northern America up to the 1980s: migration, disputes over power, personality conflicts, tensions between conservatism and progressivism, loss of uniform beliefs, and displaced hostility.[21] Redekop explains that some Canadian Mennonites migrated because they felt that the Canadian government had too much control over their education; thus, migration caused division between those who left and those who decided to remain. Disputes over power mostly happened among leaders, but also among congregations; these generated several divisions. Personality conflicts also created schisms when stubbornness or obsessive concerns could not lead Mennonites toward a solution. The schism between conservatism and progressivism stemmed from the desire of older generations to preserve their core values and views, like those pertaining to family or sexuality, with newer generations challenging them because these views did not represent their current reality. And as Mennonites were more exposed to diverse perspectives, the common lifestyle and rules that once allowed them to maintain unity did not resonate with modern Mennonites; as a result, they created different subgroups. Lastly, displaced hostility accumulated as tensions and anxiety about mainstream society were deflected within the Mennonite community. Although the main issues came from outside, Mennonites were not able to do anything about them; therefore, these hostilities were projected onto people within the community. For example, Mennonites would accuse each other of heresy, impurity, and laxity, when in fact the real cause of their anxiety and tensions came from outside of the community. In the midst of diversity, Canadian Mennonites experienced several schisms and conflicts.

Analyzing the different factors that caused schisms throughout the history of Canadian Mennonites, Redekop argues that the ethnoreligious community experienced both "structural disequilibrium" and "ideological conflict" stemming from social change and the drastic increase in diversity.[22] Patterns of immigration in Canada also changed, further increasing religious pluralism and secularization. The community sought to retain its identity while being bombarded by competing systems of thought. This required Mennonites to give a more intelligible and sophisticated reasoning for their beliefs. Again, these struggles led to various schisms and divisions.

However, despite the conflicts, Mennonites' faith and calling toward unity over the years also empowered them to collaborate with different Mennonite groups. For example, from the US side, the General Conference Mennonite Church emerged between 1847 and 1850 to unite all Mennonite groups. In 1902, Canadian Mennonite leaders in Manitoba and Saskatchewan founded the Conference of Mennonites in Central Canada; by 1932, they had incorporated churches in different provinces and changed their name to the General Conference of Mennonites in Canada (which was later changed to the Conference of Mennonites in Canada in 1959).[23] The Mennonites also began to be more involved in ecumenical dialogues from the early 1950s on. Furthermore, several Mennonite groups co-operated to found such organizations as the Mennonite Central Committee, Mennonite Mutual Aid, Mennonite Disaster Services, and several Mennonite colleges and seminaries. Moreover, in 1988, three different Mennonite groups – the Mennonite Conference of Ontario and Quebec, the Western Ontario Mennonite Conference, and the Conference of United Mennonite Churches in Ontario – came together to form the Mennonite Conference of Eastern Canada, which, in October 2001, it came to be called Mennonite Church Eastern Canada in recognition of the change of the Mennonite Church and the General Conference Mennonite Church into MC USA and MC Canada, respectively.[24]

On the cultural side, in the late 1970s, four ethnic Chinese churches joined the Conference of Mennonites in Canada.[25] From that time on, the number of non-ethnic Mennonite churches grew due to refugee-sponsorship efforts and missional work. Diversity and pluralism are still expanding within the community. Currently, of the 230 congregations that make up MC Canada, 43 worship in languages other than English or German.[26] Within MC USA, around 18 per cent are racialized Mennonites; this is largely due to evangelism and to some racialized people finding Mennonite churches to be an authentic expression of their faith.[27] As an example, the current executive director of MC USA is Glen Guyton – the first African American to serve in that position.

Theological diversity has been increasing as well. Some Mennonites have adapted to the influence of mainline churches and evangelical cultures; more women are active in leadership roles; some congregations have contemporary Christian worship music; and others have more liturgical worship forms. A more active effort toward ecumenical engagement is underway, and several interfaith dialogues are occurring. Moreover, not only are some voices advocating for same-sex marriages to be blessed by the church, they are also advocating for a greater number of LGBTQAI2+ Mennonites to be placed in church leadership roles. Through the ever-expanding nature of diversity, Mennonites are faced with new challenges and must reflect on how to maintain their core values and strive for unity while at the same time respecting difference.

Church Engagements with the World

Several points raised in this section overlap with two important themes identified above – namely, nonconformity and diversity/difference. But it is vital to examine a third theme separately here since it pertains to the two main ways in which Mennonites have intentionally engaged with the world: through missionary work and through service. Beginning with the missionary aspect, several well-known Mennonites scholars – S.F. Pannabecker, Wilbert Shenk, and Calvin Redekop, among others – agree that the early Anabaptists engaged actively in mission work and that sharing the gospel consequently became one of the Mennonites' core values.[28] The missionary engagement of lay members and the understanding that mission is the foundation of the church empowered the early Anabaptists churches to assume a missional role. However, religious persecution resulted in the suppression of these efforts, and early missionaries were forced to scatter to remote areas. Hence, Edmund Kauffman writes that "by about 1550 a great change took place among the Anabaptists. Before this time they had enthusiasm for a world mission, but after this they fled from the world and wasted their energies in the creation and application of strict rules of custom."[29] Kauffman further states that due to "continued isolation, at first caused by outside suppression and opposition but later maintained as an ideal, Mennonites were not much affected by and took little interest in what was going on in the world about them."[30] This ideal is interlinked with the Mennonite understanding of nonconformity.

Yet the suppressed spirit of mission returned, according to Regehr, when revival movements from the Protestant churches swept through

Europe and North America in the mid-nineteenth century.[31] These movements helped Mennonites rediscover the missionary nature of their faith tradition. There grew a renewed commitment to mission on the part of the church, which brought together various Mennonite groups. As a result, mission has now become an official church program in local churches, and church leaders actually find more support from church members for mission work than for educational institutions.[32] Mennonites see mission work as the highest calling of the church and as a driver of social change as well.

Kaufmann also identifies other elements, beyond the revival movements, that influenced Mennonites to actively engage in mission: their upward socio-economic mobility (which provided greater resources); the shifting circumstances in various countries that allowed and accepted Mennonite missionaries (resulting in more open and favourable settings than before); and, lastly, their superiority complex – a reaction against the earlier emphasis on inversion – which caused Mennonites to enter into missionary work more enthusiastically.[33] Not only did these factors revive their commitment to mission work, but they also provided settings and resources for Mennonite churches to advance both their home and their overseas missions. As a result of such missionary endeavours – some quite aggressive – 65 per cent of Mennonites now reside in the Global South, compared to only 35 per cent in the Global North.[34] Since 2001, 93 per cent of the growth in the global Anabaptist-Mennonite Church has occurred in Asia, Africa, and Latin America.[35] Mennonite migrations have affected this pattern as well because ethnic Mennonites migrated to some parts of the Global South. But, as Robert Suderman clarifies, this demographic change in the global Mennonite Church is largely due to missionary work.[36]

This work has shaped Mennonite identity and how Mennonites relate to one another. Redekop argues that from a sociological perspective, missionary institutions fulfill several important functions. To start, they serve as a means for Mennonites to assert their superiority, or at least equality, vis-à-vis other societies and denominations. Additionally, they provide tangible evidence of the value that Mennonites can offer the world, as indicated by the acceptance of mission work in various countries. These institutions also offer an approved avenue for individuals, particularly young people and those struggling to find a place within the Mennonite community, to connect with their fellow believers. Furthermore, they provide an opportunity for Mennonites to align with societal norms and beliefs, fostering fellowship and social cohesion. Lastly, engagement in missionary work can be seen as an acceptance of the "cultural imperialism" that has accompanied most religious systems in the West.[37]

It must be said that this interpretation is not widely shared among Mennonite scholars, and some might argue that Redekop has an impoverished view of missionary institutions, seemingly unaware of the diverse work of these organizations and the positive contributions they have made to Mennonite churches and the wider world. Yet, Redekop's description conveys an awareness of how some Mennonite groups, through their missionary work, were led to accommodate to mainline church culture, at least in their approach to missions, with some even assimilating mainline church approaches. Furthermore, Mennonites and their mission groups implicitly aligned themselves with the cultural imperialism of the West toward the Global South. While their networks and relationships with other Mennonite and Christian groups were enhanced through their missionary projects and activities – reliant as these were on global economic and political power and the colonial systems of the West – they also (whether intentionally or unintentionally) accepted, or at least acquiesced to, the cultural imperialism of the West.

Given these realities, Canadian Mennonites' active involvement in missions influenced their ethnic identity as well. Noticing how new converts from their missionary efforts sought to maintain their own cultural identities, traditions, and customs, and understanding that this was important, some Canadian Mennonites avoided imposing a strong Mennonite identity in order to make the gospel more relevant to people in their local contexts. As a result, instead of planting churches and naming them "Mennonite," or requiring new believers to sing from Mennonite hymnals, these Mennonite missionaries began to be drawn more toward new forms of evangelism that mostly focused on what would be "transmittable" in the gospel as a "supra-cultural," purely "spiritual" ethos. Since they saw this gospel as above culture, in their missionary work they did not consider the cultural and ethnic features of the people to whom they were preaching. According to Regehr, this caused the Mennonites to abandon not only their ethnic identity and cultural traits, but also their understanding of holistic discipleship, mission, and lifestyle, which are crucial aspects of Mennonite faith and tradition.[38]

A strange dynamic also began to take shape between local churches and "mission fields" as a result of this missionary engagement. For the Mennonites, local churches were places of worship and fellowship, communities in which they could celebrate different life stages and find encouragement in moments of vulnerability. At the same time, mission fields were places that Mennonites supported financially and where they sent their people to collaborate with local communities, usually those who are poor. Problems can occur when those who have historically been the objects of mission work then become active participants and leaders in the church, especially when such people have been traditionally perceived according to a unidirectional (non-mutual) charity model that reflects an "us" versus "them" view of the world. Regehr explains this dynamic in the following terms:

> Canadian Mennonites were generally upwardly mobile, but missions were usually designed for the poor, the shiftless, the underprivileged, and the disadvantaged. Concern about, and help for, impoverished and oppressed people who might disrupt the established order has always been fashionable among Canadian elites. It has not, however, been fashionable to bring such people into direct fellowship or into relationships of equality unless they also accept the religious and cultural values and practices of the elite.[39]

The newly converted in Canada were required to assimilate to the dominant culture and lifestyle that existed within the Mennonite Church in order to engage more deeply in fellowship. This goes against the larger effort of becoming an intercultural church. The "believed" aspect of the missional church for which Barrett and Suderman advocate tries to overcome this "experienced" polarization between local churches and mission fields: they argue that all places are missional fields, that no place is non-missional, and that we must merge our daily lives and our work in mission fields. By advocating for such a view, they are opposing the practice of othering people in the "mission field" and the paternalistic attitude of the "sending" church.

In addition to missionary work, another way that Canadian Mennonites have engaged with the world is through the Mennonite Central Committee (MCC). The MCC was formed by several major Mennonite organizations in Northern America on 27 September 1920 in Chicago, Illinois. Through MCC, the groups sought to collaborate together in relief works, especially assisting other Mennonites who were suffering in the Soviet Union and other European countries, as well as helping refugee Mennonites to settle in Northern America.[40] While they actively collaborated in several ways with the US Central Committee, Canadian Mennonites later formed their own office in Canada in 1944. Then, in 1963, Mennonite Central Committee Canada was formed through the union of seven inter-Mennonite service organizations. In the years since, the organization has worked co-operatively with MCC.[41] Initially, MCC Canada was an organization that primarily served its own people, European or North American Mennonites; but as its members learned of other people suffering from war, starvation, and persecution, they began to serve diverse groups and people from other countries.

The formation of MCC Canada not only fostered collaboration among various Mennonite groups and organizations, it also provided "an effective and unified voice for Canadian Mennonites when they spoke to governments or to the public about their peace position."[42] MCC Canada was and is the organization through which Canadian Mennonites engage with the wider world, including politics. Since 1963, the organization has expanded its activities to focus more on development rather than simply relief work; it has also created a voluntary service program that operates across the country, and it advocates for social issues and concerns through its office in Ottawa.

In his sociological analysis of MCC Canada, Redekop identifies at least seven functions of the organization. First, it is an effective vehicle for Mennonites service, since it is widely accepted by various Mennonite groups and it maintains the biblical mandate to serve the poor. Second, it serves as a mechanism by which Mennonites can engage with the world in a manner supported by their fellow Mennonites; hence, while the people interact with the world, their faith and identity are protected under the umbrella of MCC Canada. Third, the organization provides a platform through which Mennonites can attempt various experiments and try out new programs that would otherwise be impossible for local churches to offer, either due to a lack of resources, or because of the reluctance of individual church members. Fourth – and building on the point just raised – it is a place where new creative ideas for social engagement can be expressed and communicated, as it is a safer and more open space than some conservative churches. Fifth, because the organization is not involved explicitly in either mission work or theological engagement, it allows for broader co-operation among Mennonite groups and organizations. Sixth, it functions as a symbol and expression of the relevance and influence of Mennonite faith in the world and shows that Mennonites are not an enclaved people. Lastly, it also serves as a centre of identity for the Mennonite community, a space where various important themes and topics of Mennonite concerns are in dialogue. Even those who are not connected to local churches feel a strong sense of community through MCC Canada.[43] MCC Canada is a significant and highly regarded organization among those Mennonites who actively engage with the world; it serves as a channel through which various Mennonite organizations and local churches can co-operate to serve people in need and be socially transformative.

Despite this history of support and collaboration, MCC Canada has faced several challenges and criticisms, from both conservative and liberal groups. And internal struggles within the organization are increasing as its membership becomes more diverse. One important criticism relates to the claim of some members that MCC Canada does not reflect the church's ethnic and racial diversity in its own leadership and staffing composition, or in the issues for which it advocates. The organization has also received complaints of racial discrimination and accusations that it is not a welcoming place for non-ethnic Mennonites.[44] While some effort has been made to restructure the organization so that it might be more inclusive, some people have opposed this "equity agenda" for fear that it would create further division by accentuating members' differences.

Although there is space for improvement in MCC Canada, as Esther Epp-Tiessen asserts, "it drew people out of their comfort zones and built relationships across the divides. It was at its best when these people-to-people encounters were mutually transformative – and where giving and receiving flowed in both directions."[45] MCC Canada serves not only as a channel for Mennonites to engage with the world and to transform society, but also as an educational vehicle. Through the organization,

Mennonites have learned more about global issues and the concerns of society, and as a result, Mennonites have gained a new understanding of the world, themselves, and how to collaborate with each other and express their faith in a relevant way. Indeed, MCC Canada has been transformative for Canadian Mennonites.

As is clear from this brief analysis of the "experienced" church, MC Canada has undergone numerous changes. It still faces several challenges that push the church to work continuously work toward transformation. Canadian Mennonite scholars and feminists such as Lydia Harder, Carol Penner, and Marlene Epp point out that the church is still a patriarchal, male-centred institution. Others note that heteronormativity is dominant. Still other voices problematize Mennonite ethnicity and the fact that the "traditional" ethnic identities – particularly Swiss, Dutch, German, and Russian – remain dominant.[46] Along with the issue of ethnicity, some people emphasize race as a matter of critical importance because people of colour perceive whiteness as a barrier to their full inclusion in the community and because local churches still remain racially and ethnically segregated.[47]

Although we have no recent quantitative research for MC Canada, in 2007, Conrad Kanagy surveyed the churches comprising MC USA to understand the church's racial and ethnic composition and to identify the areas where it would need to grow and improve.[48] He discovered that many white Mennonites, including non-ethnic Mennonites, have little awareness of the increasing number of racial and other ethnic Mennonites. Also, he realized that these Mennonites feel alienated from the dominant group and the power structures of the church.[49] For this reason, finding fresh and creative ways of welcoming these minority groups into the church is the "most important challenge and opportunity facing the denomination. But if new patterns of relating, including the redistribution of power and resources, do not develop, I suspect that some Racial/Ethnic members will leave the denomination. If they do, the church will have missed perhaps its last and best opportunity for renewal."[50] Kanagy made this statement to MC USA, but his message is certainly relevant to MC Canada as well. Canadian Mennonite churches will need to find ways to be more inclusive of racialized and "non-ethnic" Mennonites and redistribute power and opportunities fairly with the wider community. This endeavour, in my view, will help the church become intercultural.

In this chapter, I provided a broad-stroke narrative of the "experienced" church of MC Canada and examined how Mennonite peoplehood was negotiated among members, drawing on sociological analyses offered by Mennonite historians and sociologists. I focused on three interrelated themes: (1) how Mennonites' understanding of nonconformity has changed over time; (2) how Canadian Mennonites have dealt with diversity and difference; and (3) how the church's engagement with the world has shifted within the Mennonite canopy. These themes are related because they help to explain how Mennonites sought to maintain one of their core beliefs, nonconformity, in the context of growing diversity and difference within their community and in their engagement with the world throughout their presence in Canada. Examining the "experienced" church is crucial to understanding the difference between the church as doctrine and as the church human community. As the "experienced" church shifted, Mennonites were forced to adjust their sense of the "believed" church – for example, by engaging with the world more directly and by exposing the gaps between the church's ideals and its current context. At the same time, this examination helps to show how Canadian Mennonite churches have developed historically, and what is necessary to empower them to become more intercultural.

We can observe that, as the Mennonites faced various challenges, negotiating these meant re-examining their values and identities, and doing so in a way that balanced old with new, maintaining tradition yet accommodating to change. Some of the transformations Canadian Mennonites underwent were necessary for the community to continue with its faith traditions and to survive as a unified whole; otherwise, it could have been assimilated into the evangelical stream of Christianity, or simply remained an ethnic immigrant community. In this process, Mennonite theology, ways of living, and engagement with the world have been transformed. Even though the growing diversity and difference within the church has led at various points to conflict, division, and schism, Mennonites have also found ways to unite and collaborate with each other. New challenges are still ahead, however. Critical voices continue to highlight issues pertaining to gender, race, and ethnicity issues and call on the church to be more inclusive and welcoming. As Mennonites did in the past when they encountered conflict, they need to continue to struggle with these new issues whenever their existing Mennonite beliefs and interpretations do not provide easy solutions. This book is meant to contribute to this process. It is an urgent task, because church leaders are wondering how they can lead in a context of growing diversity and in which racialized and "non-ethnic" members feel excluded and marginalized. With these concerns in mind, I offer guidelines for engaging these issues so that churches may become intercultural through beliefs and practices rooted in the Anabaptist-Mennonite tradition.

Part 1 has examined the "believed" and "experienced" church – the church as both a theological and a sociological reality. In concluding this section of the book, I offer three remarks. First, in both the "believed" and the "experienced" church, one can observe that the Mennonite community endorses a more active involvement in society than has traditionally been the case, advocating for greater engagement with the world. Both the "believed" and the "experienced" church stress a Mennonite identity that is capable of accommodating itself to the changes happening in society and that moves away from stricter versions of nonconformity. Mennonites emphasize this need for engagement, which is important both as they live in pluralistic society, and as they witness and do missional work.

Second, the three visions of the "believed" church assessed in chapter 1 help the community to aspire be more involved in the world and provide reasons why and how Mennonites should engage. From the traditional view that the church needs to withdraw from society, the messianic community exhorts an evangelical nonconformist approach, and the missional church encourages a nonconformed engagement; the shalom church advocates not only for the missional work of the church, but also for social responsibility. Nevertheless, the theological perspective alone is not enough for Mennonites to interact in society, since the "believed" church does not address specific details like how to collaborate with governments, how to relate with other religious organizations that work for social justice, or how to resist certain policies and laws. My analysis of the "experienced" church shows how the wisdom gained from quotidian interaction, collaboration, and communal work with different groups, along with perspectives from other areas of study, have informed how Mennonites should pursue a greater engagement with society. This "experienced" church has affected the "believed" church, and both of them are dialectically interrelated. The "experienced" church that went through numerous changes offered valuable insights and new possibilities for change, and these understandings informed and reshaped the church's ecclesiologies. For example, in the case of the shalom church, Friesen integrates several insights from different fields of study and the experience gained from MCC.[51] Furthermore, Berry integrates the experiences of traditionally marginalized groups, like women and African Americans, into her theology.

Third, as one could have predicted, it is true that the unity Yoder describes is not fully realized in the Mennonite community; the reality and the practices of Mennonites have not caught up to the aspirations of the "believed" church. Nonetheless, what the "believed" church lacks is a careful examination of the much more complicated role that unity plays in the lived experience of Canadian Mennonites. Hence, I propose yet further negotiation as the "experienced" church invites theological changes, compelling visions of the "believed" church to readjust and open toward new realities. Yoder mentions the complicated dimensions of culture, economy, and social status among believers, but the "experienced" church shows that there are many more types of difference, including race, politics, ability, and power. As a result, Mennonites must find ways to strive toward unity through the lived experience of the people, cautiously considering the relationships among individuals, social groups, and organizations in their particular contexts.

Based on the last two paragraphs, one can see the importance of both the "believed" and the "experienced" church. The "believed" church inspires the community to live out what it believes, and the "experienced" church informs believers' ecclesiology so that it can incorporate new insights and understandings. The resulting theological perspective may therefore be empowering, relevant, and appropriate. However, in some cases, the two can be out of step with each other and therefore cause harm. For instance, the traditional concept of nonconformity, which was subject to different criteria based on one's gender, was used to silence women. At the same time, a crucial theological reality of mission and witnessing was dismissed and forgotten when the Mennonites experienced severe persecution. As a result, the church, which maintains both a theological and a socio-historical reality, needs to hold on to both of these aspects and find ways to faithfully live out these theological ideals as rooted in their particular socio-historical contexts. An understanding of Canadian society is crucial if Mennonite communities in the country are to more faithfully embody their faith in the modern context. Having a better sense of society can also inform our theology of the church, which in turn will allow us to offer concepts and theories that are appropriate to the praxes of the people. To that end, in part 2 I explore one important aspect of Canadian society, multiculturalism, and how difference and diversity are dealt through official policy.

PART TWO

Context and Theology

In part 1, I explored Mennonite peoplehood in Canada by comparing the "believed" and the "experienced" church. There, I argued that a constant shaping and reshaping of the "believed" and the "experienced" church – a sort of dialectical interplay between the two – is crucial to addressing the gap between them and to creating an ecclesiology that is relevant, appropriate, and empowering. This kind of ecclesiology relates to the lives and experiences of believers (relevant); resonates with the Bible, theological sources, and the context of the believers (appropriate); and guides believers to act, make decisions, and live out their faith concretely in their social location (empowering). In an attempt to provide a theo-ethical model of this shaping process, chapter 4 focuses on how difference has been understood and grappled with in Canadian society. Setting the stage for this focus, chapter 3 examines the nature of contextual theology to highlight the correlation between context and theology, and to explore how culture, ethnicity, race, and faith are interconnected. These interconnections are particularly important for this work because they inform how Canadian Mennonites, within their ethnocultural and racial identities, can become an intercultural church, which will be the main focus of part 3. This discussion draws insights primarily from the work of Kathryn Tanner and Néstor Medina, whose research explicitly discusses culture and theology and addresses how these are intrinsically related with each other. Then, based on the six different models of contextual theology identified by Stephen Bevans, I note that not all contextual theologies are liberative, and suggest that a liberative lens is imperative when doing theology. I conclude that the best ideals from the Mennonite perspective emerge from a liberative approach and require a combination of Bevans's anthropological, praxis, and countercultural models.[1]

Building on these insights, chapter 4 examines how difference is dealt with through the policies of multiculturalism in Canada and ultimately what these policies aspire to do. Relying upon the work of several Canadian critical social theorists, I discuss how multiculturalism operates to oppress and exploit marginalized groups, especially through systemic racism and settler colonialism. As an alternative way to engage with diversity and difference in Canada's multicultural context, the latter part of the chapter further analyzes the concept of interculturality, noting how the term is used in different geographical locations and fields of studies, including theology. This overview then helps to formulate a foundational principle of interculturality from an Anabaptist-Mennonite perspective: shalom.

3

Culture, Ethnicity, Race, and Faith

In Western societies, Christian theology has until recently generally been understood to be universally true, unchanging, and objective, emerging purely from the Bible and tradition. Some Christian leaders thought that their role was simply to speak that truth, assuming that it would naturally make sense to the receivers. However, theologians are now more aware that one's particular social location deeply influences one's theology. As a result, they have come increasingly to adopt various methods to "self-consciously" harness this awareness to construct theological relevance, appropriateness, and empowerment. This method of theologizing is called contextual theology; its core insight is that theology has always been deeply influenced by its surrounding environment. Angie Pears states that contextual theology "explicitly places the recognition of the contextual nature of theology at the forefront of the theological process."[1] While all theological perspectives are contextual insofar as they are shaped by the context in which they are produced, contextual theology differentiates between those views that intentionally integrate contextual factors into theo-ethical thinking and those that do so only indirectly and without self-awareness. One reason this discourse has emerged is to challenge and reject traditional theologies that make a claim to universal truth and assume a widespread applicability, and which therefore dismiss those theological perspectives that do not align with traditional views. Since these theologies are fixed, universal, and objective, they become irrelevant, inappropriate, and disempowering because they do not resonate with the life and experience of local communities.[2] They can also function oppressively vis-à-vis marginalized people because their voices can be ignored and silenced, as feminist, Black, Latin American liberation, post-colonial, and other kinds of contextual theologians would assert. Contextual theologians resist understanding theology as a "once and for all" enterprise, and so they construct perspectives that are explicitly informed and transformed by local contexts.

What does context mean to contextual theologians then? According to Sigurd Bergmann, the word "context" is derived from philology and refers to those elements that surround a text, specifically

> the parts of a text that precede and follow the text in question and which are of importance for its understanding ... The linguistic meaning of context can be transferred to other fields. Today the word also denotes the particular social, cultural and ecological situation within which a course of events takes place. A theological text, for instance, comes into being within a wider context, that is, it is determined by the traditions and circumstances that have an effect on the complex situation of the author and the reader.[3]

Bergmann helps us to understand that when we read scripture or construct our theological view, there always is a context or situation that shapes our way of thinking, feeling, and responding. As Stephen Bevans argues, our reality is not just "out there," rather it is mediated and interpreted from our own "particular horizon and in our own particular thought forms."[4] As a result, there is no objective or neutral theo-ethical view. Walter Hollenweger supports this observation:

> All theologies – including the biblical ones – are contextually conditioned. There is no pure gospel. The gospel appears to us *per definitionem* in an incarnate form. We have no access to a gospel outside its incarnation in culture, language, thought patterns, etc. That is why there is nothing wrong with theology being contextually conditioned. But to call a gospel which is heavily dependent on a capitalist society and on Aristotelian philosophy the "pure gospel" or even "the full gospel" is a grave overstatement. It usually takes others to show us how conditioned, parochial and ideologically captive our own theology is. Even if once we could ignore such voices, now we can no longer do so.[5]

The gospel of peace preached by Jesus seeks to liberate people from all kinds of oppression and violence and guide them toward an alternative way of living, which is shalom. The gospel is good news that empowers everyone to thrive, especially those who are marginalized. While it is universal and transcultural, ultimately it is human beings – living as they do in a limited time and space – who are the ones interpreting and embodying that truth in particular ways, discerning how it should be applied in each specific context. Consequently, there is no transcendental understanding of the gospel that can be applied uniformly to all contexts. Theologies, which are elaborated by people, can only be conditional and contextual. If this is true, then, one cannot state that one's theology is the one pure and right belief. The tension between the gospel as both universal and particular is never resolvable. Any theology needs to attend to both its particular/local/contextual and its universal/global/transcendental dimensions because the context always shapes one's theological articulation. And yet, at the same time, theology cannot be simply a product of one's surroundings. Recognizing the universal aspect of theology does not mean that there is only one true theology, and that all the rest are wrong; rather, it means that theology speaks beyond one's own context because the gospel of Jesus Christ is good news for all people.

A question then arises: What exactly are those contextual factors that deeply influence one's faith and theology? Bergmann highlights ten key factors: geography, gender, ethnic affiliations, culturally constructed power, class, economy, ecology, generation, education, and place.[6] Bevans similarly explains that faith and theology are the product of a combination of several factors such as a person's or group's personal life, cultural context, gender, social location, geography, and the reality their experience of social change.[7] He recognizes that culture and society are constantly shifting, and that this reality profoundly influences what and how people experience.

Based on the analysis offered by Bergmann and Bevans, it is clear that culture and ethnicity are both crucially important factors that shape faith and theology. Since the primary focus of this book is culture, ethnicity, and race, this chapter concentrates specifically on these contextual factors so as to more adequately address how they intersect with theology. Although the category of race is not on the list suggested by Bergmann and Bevans, I emphasize it here because racial identity deeply influences how people live and theologize in Canada. This chapter does not attempt an exhaustive survey of theories of culture, ethnicity, and race; rather, it explores these topics strategically with the aim of laying a basic foundation for understanding the intercultural work of Canadian Mennonites.

Culture is a complicated concept, one for which there is no single, satisfying definition. Besides, as Néstor Medina, a Canadian theologian, observes, it traditionally carries "inherent Eurocentric baggage, establishing European cultures as the normative highest expressions of human 'development' in a hierarchy of cultures."[8] In *Theories of Culture*, Kathryn Tanner gives an in-depth explanation of the historical uses of the word "culture" in France, Germany, and Britain. While the term was understood differently in each country, there nevertheless was a general agreement that each group thought their culture was superior.[9] T.J. Gorringe also explains how the concept of culture grew in Europe out of European ideas of civilization.[10] Linking culture with civilization in order to establish the superiority of one culture over another has created harmful and chauvinistic beliefs that that "cultured" people have progressed and advanced further in all areas of social life than "uncivilized" and "uncultured" people.

A modern anthropological view – as advanced in the work of Clifford Geertz, Claude Lévi-Strauss, Victor Turner, Ruth Benedict, and others – challenges the normative assumptions that underly cultural hierarchies and the supposed ethnocentric superiority of "European" civilization. These scholars, as Tanner notes, have established several key understandings of culture: that it's a universal human phenomenon, but not uniform across all people or groups; that it varies significantly among cultural groups and encompasses their entire way of life; that it's associated with social consensus and shapes human nature; that cultures are human constructs and thus contingent; and, finally, that culture implies social determinism, as societies play a pivotal role in shaping their members. This perspective challenges Eurocentric notions of culture and emphasizes the diversity and complexity of human societies.[11]

Such insights shed new light on the claim that culture is ubiquitous and that all human beings belong to a cultural group (or cultural groups) with its own patterns of meaning and practices that are material, linguistic, and ritual. Broadly speaking, modern and anthropological descriptions of culture, beginning with the work of Johann Gottfried von Herder, moved toward the "local," recognizing that every people and nation have a distinctive culture, and that cultural factors shape and form one's social identity, one's sense of the meaning of life, and one's perception of one's surroundings.

Still, in a generally postmodern perspective informed by post-colonial theory, Tanner perceives limits to the modern anthropological view of culture. She critiques these perspectives for their lack of awareness of the culture-shaping forces of nationalism, colonialism, and the powerful influence of intellectual elites, all of which play a crucial role in determining how power and economic resources are distributed, and who is considered normal, and who deviant, within a cultural group.[12] Furthermore, she points out that modern anthropologists assume that culture is made up of "self-contained and clearly bounded units, internally consistent and unified wholes of beliefs and values simply transmitted to every member of their respective groups as principles of social order."[13] Writing from a postmodern perspective, however, she asserts that cultures are always in the process of being shaped, and that they are not internally consistent wholes. Though there may be some degree of consensus within a culture, it is extremely limited since each member of a cultural group can have different points of view.[14] Moreover, cultures are fluid and porous, meaning that they always open toward change and are constantly being influenced by their larger surroundings. Cultures may cross boundaries without endangering their distinctiveness. "The distinctiveness of cultural identity is therefore not a product of isolation; it is not a matter of a culture's being simply self-generated, pure and unmixed; it is not a matter of 'us' vs 'them.' Cultural identity becomes, instead, a hybrid, relational affair, something that lives between as much as within cultures."[15] In other words, cultures are neither static nor complete. As our understanding of culture moves from a colonial paradigm to a modern one, and then to a postmodern one, culture becomes much more difficult to describe. Hence, even though there are numerous definitions of the word, no one meaning is fully satisfactory. This complicates the task of identifying cultures as neatly circumscribed wholes.

Based on the points made by Tanner, then, one can argue that culture informs people of the appropriate ways to organize their lives, how to behave, what to eat, and so on. It provides a lens through which people interpret their experiences and the surrounding reality, including certain symbols, rituals, and gestures. It also shapes our evaluations of others' behaviours and actions. Thus, culture informs how each individual interprets all the actions and reactions around them, from the smallest to the largest. Moreover, culture is always particular rather than universal, and several world views or conceptual frameworks exist in the world. As a result, there is no vantage point from which to claim that one cultural view is the only valid one and that all others are invalid.

As Tanner notes, these conceptual frameworks or world views are always changing. Néstor Medina likewise states that cultures are

> Porous, open-ended, unfinished, and fluid. That does not take away from their totalizing function providing members of a group with a sense of overall coherence. By coherence I do not mean that all aspects of any given cultural tradition fit neatly together or that there are no internal contradictions in any given cultural "system." Rather, cultures provide members with a sense of totality, a sense of coherence, a meta-frame that explains – albeit limitedly – all aspects of life and reality. Cultures encompass the entire gamut of social phenomena in human collectives.[16]

According to Medina, while culture is an unfinished product with diverse voices and views, it nevertheless contains certain systemic properties that help people interpret and understand their lives and the surrounding reality. For instance, although Canadian culture has gone through various changes, and it is difficult to name specific cultural aspects that are essentially "Canadian," we can identify certain features that have come to be understood in common, albeit not with complete coherence.

Probing more deeply, it is also worth noting how ideologies connect to and function within culture. Tanner has pointed out that modern anthropological understandings of culture do not include an awareness of how various ideologies like nationalism and colonialism have shaped cultures, though it must be said she did not engage with these categories in depth. Helpfully, Gorringe takes up the point by offering a more robust discourse on culture that includes ideologies and power structures. He asserts that "ideas, beliefs, philosophies, [and] theologies," which can be subsumed under the larger notion of ideology, are deeply embedded in culture.[17] Furthermore, these ideologies, especially the dominant ones, support and justify existing hegemonic social forces. Together, hegemonic ideas shape "what counts in society and what does not, what is at the centre and what is at the margins, which voices are heard and which silenced."[18] As a result, they help perpetuate profound inequalities in the areas of class, gender, and race. To comprehend how hegemonic ideas are embedded in a culture, Gorringe explains that hegemony exists through the consent of the general population, and not through "rule."[19] People in a dominant position constantly propagate their ideologies and influence the general population to accept them as "rational, reasonable, credible, indeed sayable or thinkable."[20] In other words, the resulting ideas are not natural phenomena but products of meaning in culture (what matters and is "normal"). Although Gorringe offers new insights into the connection between culture and hegemony, he does not point out that when there is a power differential, a fully consenting relationship between the people in power and the general population is impossible. Hence, when observing cultural practices, it is imperative to critically analyze not only how certain ideologies are operative but also how power imbalances are structured.

This deliberately narrow discussion of culture notes what culture encompasses, how it is constantly changing, that it is neither monolithic nor uniform, and how ideology and culture are interconnected. I now focus on the second contextual factor that influences our faith: ethnicity. This is a significant aspect of this book because Mennonite identity is often conflated with ethnicity, and this results in certain exclusionary and marginalizing practices. How is ethnicity both similar to and different from culture? The two share several overlapping aspects, and so the lines separating them are often quite blurry; however, in cultural anthropology, what is understood as culture is in fact macro-culture, a larger umbrella, while ethnicity is micro-culture. "Micro-culture" refers to the lifestyle of a group of people who, in general, share a set of values and beliefs related to the macro-culture, but who are bonded together more closely by "similar experiences, traits, values, or in some cases, histories."[21] Furthermore, micro-cultures commonly can be differentiated from the larger culture by race, history, geographical location, language, or religion. In general, an ethnic group is understood to be a people who are related through "common filiation, or blood, [and] whose members also usually feel a sense of attachment to a particular place, a history, and a culture."[22] Yet, careful scrutiny shows that ethnicity is actually deeply influenced by political, social, and economic factors, and is also produced and governed by ideology. This means that ethnicity, like culture, is socially constructed, that it is "established by time, tempered by space, and conditioned by social interaction."[23] For instance, the understanding of ethnic Mennonite identity that Mennonites had fifty years ago in Manitoba is different from how contemporary Mennonites in Chaco, Paraguay, perceive themselves, because their socio-political, economical, geographical, historical, and linguistic environments are so different.

Ethnic consciousness – the awareness of one's ethnic identity and belonging – is also socially constructed. It can emerge among a group of people who may not be genetically or even culturally connected. For example, the majority of South Koreans consider themselves a homogeneous ethnic group; and yet, there are, in fact, numerous inter-ethnic and/or interracial families in the country, and Koreans are deeply influenced by Chinese, Japanese, and Western cultures. Ethnic identity is fluid, porous, and hybrid, and its core markers may change over time. However, because of the collective ethnic identity that people have developed, both intentionally and unintentionally, "a certain consensus within the group about what constitutes it as such and differentiates it from other groups,"[24] ethnicity tends to be viewed as an identity marker that is less fluid than culture. As a result, there is a stronger emphasis on who is "in" and who is "out."

In the Canadian context, the term "ethnicity" is often used to describe racialized groups, who are then depicted as people at the margins of the "centres of power, wealth, and status of Canadian society."[25] The term is rarely used to describe Euro-Canadians, at least those born in the country, as if they do not belong to a particular ethnic group. This demonstrates that hierarchical and normalizing notions of "culture" still operate, although Euro-Canadians may refer to their "ethnic origins" when describing their ancestors. Since they assume a normative position of privilege, they often do not perceive themselves as linked to any ethnic group. As a result, Euro-Canadians are considered "mainstream" or "non-ethnic" Canadians. This language conveys a distinct bias that normalizes linguistic processes of social codification that are distinctly Eurocentric – and which end up privileging Euro-Canadians. Nonetheless, if "ethnicity" means communities of people "bound together by a common historical narrative, genetic heritage, language, culture, food, and to a very large extent, religion," then, as scholars like Paul Bramadat and David Seljak assert, Canadians of British and French heritage should be considered members of these ethnic groups as well.[26]

In light of this understanding of culture and ethnicity, we can assert a few claims pertaining to Mennonite culture and ethnicity. First, there is no internally consistent understanding of what Mennonite culture is. Within Mennonite communities, Mennonite culture is understood in various – and sometimes contradictory – ways. Consequently, instead of referring to Mennonite culture in the singular, we should actually speak of Mennonite cultures. Second, Mennonite cultures have been changing under the influence of their surroundings; and a diverse array of voices are involved in the process of shaping and reshaping Mennonite cultures. As a result, there are no "pure" Mennonite cultures. Even though the current understanding of Mennonite cultures has been moulded to a great extent by Mennonites of Swiss, Russian, German, or Dutch backgrounds, this does not mean that these cultures are "pure" and that they should continue to be described as such. As people from various ethnic backgrounds join Mennonite peoplehood, naturally, Mennonite cultures will be reshaped by these newcomers. When cultures change, the predominant group might experience a sense of loss: this shift is normal, and it should be neither feared nor resisted. But, of course, cultural change take years, sometimes decades. Third, faced with either maintaining the former ways or accepting newer approaches, generally, the dominant group use their power and authorities to define Mennonite cultures to create consistency, clarity, and uniformity. Yet, in so doing, they constrict the range of possible Mennonite identities and exclude the voices of people who do not agree with the dominant group, people who generally possess less power and influence. Fourth, as with culture, there is no "pure" Mennonite ethnicity as it is always in the process of being changed. The current ethnic identity of the Mennonites will no doubt take different forms fifty or a hundred years from today. At present, among ethnic Mennonites, there are numerous interracial and inter-ethnic families. While people with different skin colour and physical appearance might have "Mennonite names," they are no longer "pure" Swiss, German, Russian, or Dutch Mennonites. Mennonite ethnicities today are varied, and they will be even more diverse in the future. Nonetheless, it is the present dominant ethnic consciousness that continually highlights European heritage and repeatedly produces narratives based on the people of such background; consequently, these dominant narratives shape and form Mennonite identities. As a result, this consciousness, which is blind to other existing ethnicities, excludes Mennonites who do not have European heritage, even those with mixed heritage, such as Dutch Indonesian or Swiss Paraguayan Mennonites.

Another factor that needs to be examined is race. Like culture and ethnicity, race is also socially constructed. Michael Banton explains that the idea of race has gone through at least three phases in the Western society. The first occurred during the eighteenth century in Europe, where race was simply a tool of classification used by natural scientists to explain the different lineages of humankind. However, even in this early phase, the concept of race was influenced by the colonial context. The classification of different peoples was not value-free but was embedded in the colonial agenda, which sought to justify the subjugation and exploitation of non-European peoples. The second phase happened during the nineteenth century when natural historians used the concept to categorize people into distinct biological types in order to create hierarchies of race. The differences among various races were considered permanent and universal, and were in turn used to explain the physical, moral, intellectual, cultural, social, and economic differences among peoples. This shift was the outcome of the intersection of colonialism and science, further entrenching racial hierarchies to legitimize colonial domination. The third phase is ongoing today; it began in twentieth century when pseudo-scientific racial theories were discredited and dismissed, and so race became widely accepted as a socially constructed phenomenon.[27]

Carl James defines race as a socially constructed classification of people based on the "historical and geographical context of individual experience."[28] He asserts that the meaning of race is not "fixed," but is instead influenced by historical, political, cultural, social, and geographic factors, because who is thought to belong to a given racial category depends on context.

James writes that racism is the "uncritical acceptance of a negative social definition of a colonized or subordinate group, typically identified by physical features."[29] As a result, it creates, explains, and perpetuates inequalities. The key component of racism is power "in terms of influence that is supported by ideological, economical, political, social and cultural conditions of the society."[30] Through this power, racism can become institutional (wherein institutions enact differential treatment based on people's race) and structural (wherein a social system is justified in its allocation of racial groups to particular lower categories and class locations).

In the Canadian context, racism is based on white supremacy. Kathy Hogarth and Wendy Fletcher explain that racism in Canada is mobilized to achieve two particular ends: the colonization and removal of Indigenous people, and the management and control of immigrants who "fall outside of the 'Euro-decent Caucasian' classification, who are marginalized upon arrival in their new country."[31] These racist practices continue to be promulgated by white "Euro-Canadians" and informed by white "racial and cultural prejudice and discrimination, supported by institutional power and authority, [and] used to the advantage of Whites and the disadvantage of peoples of Color."[32] "White supremacy" does not simply describe a hatred of non-whites; as Robin DiAngelo asserts, it is a descriptive term used to "capture the all-encompassing centrality and assumed superiority of people defined and perceived as white and the practices based on this assumption."[33] Rather than referring to individual white people, it is related to an "overarching political, economic, and social system of domination" perpetuated by white people.[34] Of course, this does not mean that all white people have similar experiences. Depending on one's social location and cultural context, one's experience of whiteness will differ. For example, some early twentieth-century discourses on immigration stereotyped certain kinds of Europeans as "less desirable," like Polish, Italian, and Irish people.[35] Interestingly, some of these less desirable white groups were later included in the category of "whiteness" in Canada – and among them were the Mennonites. Mennonites with German heritage did experience discrimination during the Second World War due to anti-German sentiments among the population, but this discrimination was based on their cultural background rather than their race. This fact notwithstanding, these groups received explicit favour in the form of social rights and privileges. Indeed, white settler Mennonites were given a significant amount of land in Manitoba and Saskatchewan by the Canadian government.

Connecting these insights and descriptions of culture, ethnicity, and race with the contextual nature of theology, I argue that one's race, ethnicity, and culture profoundly influence one's religious conviction and faith. Humans are thoroughly interpretive beings: people are formed by a language (or languages) and set of practices that inform and shape how they "see" the world, their priorities, their values, etc. Culture, ethnicity, and race, then, necessarily factor into how and why the "gospel" is significant. For example, it is no accident that during the Plague Europeans created Gothic images of Christ suffering, or that in the modern era people in sub-Saharan Africa tend to view Jesus as a proto-ancestor. This realization can lead toward two significant outcomes. First, it can enable people to resist theological views that claim to embody the ultimate, universal, fixed, singular, or unchanging beliefs and truths. Second, it can animate believers to actively listen to other theological views and enter into dialogue with them. Christians who recognize that their understanding of God is limited build community among people of different backgrounds. They trust that cultural, ethnic, and racial groups other than their own can shed new light on their understanding of God and what it means to work toward peace and justice. As limited human beings, Christians need to engage with each other to have a fuller picture of God and the world. This awareness can encourage greater intercultural, ecumenical, and interfaith dialogue. But before striving toward an intercultural and ecumenical theology, we must first know how to do contextual theology that resonates and empowers Christians to live out our beliefs faithfully in our social locations and ethnocultural and racial contexts. Thus, in the next section, I examine more closely how to theologize in a liberative and contextual manner from a Mennonite perspective.

Contextual and Liberative Theology

If contextual factors profoundly influence theology, then how should we explicitly account for our context within our theologies? Moreover, what is an appropriate way of doing contextual theology? Does our theology always have to support our cultural practices? By focusing too much on context, might we end up uncritically identifying with our context as if it is some sort of universal norm? In an attempt to answer these questions, Stephen Bevans describes six different models of contextual theology as exemplified in Christian history. In addition to Bevans, several other theologians and missiologists – among them Robert Schreiter, James Woodward, Stephen Pattison, Sigurd Bergmann, and Angie Pears – carefully examine the contextual nature of theologies and how contexts and theologies mutually influence each other. Among them, I find Bevans's book *Models of Contextual Theology* quite useful since it maps out various contextual theologies and how they are related. Furthermore, his models fit well with this project because his understanding of culture and context aligns with the descriptions of culture that I have explained earlier in this chapter. Drawing on his models, I can then further develop my contextual and liberative theology and explain what this entails here and in subsequent chapters.

Bevan's six models – what he calls the translation, anthropological, praxis, synthetic, transcendental, and countercultural models – are heuristic devices, imaginative portrayals to help identify, explain, and account for observable patterns. Each offers a different way of "theologizing that takes a particular context seriously, and so each represents a distinct theological starting point and distinct theological presuppositions."[36] Some models intersect or coexist with others. My analysis of the six is deliberatively succinct, although each model deserves more nuance, and I am aware of the complexity of each. This simple overview, however, functions strategically to situate my approach and further examine the liberative perspective.

Briefly stated, the translation model understands the core gospel, the truth, the unchanging message, as supra-contextual and culture-free. Hence, when the "naked" gospel is introduced in a new context, this message should be translated into contextually appropriate terms so that it resonates with the listeners. This model takes seriously the Christian message by prioritizing the gospel and considering it the norm of culture, since it is divine revelation. However, it underemphasizes the fact that the message itself is culturally laden, that the gospel one knows is already an interpretation informed by one's particular cultural context. The gospel is incarnational, given in time and place, and not a disembodied, abstract message. Thus, people of faith have to wrestle with and discern communally how God's message is gospel to them.

The anthropological model understands that scripture and Christian tradition are culturally conditioned, and that one's context can offer insights that can help in reinterpreting these two sources. This model centres human experience and incorporates the human reality in the interpretation of the gospel. It also emphasizes the goodness of all creation. This model affirms cultural context, but it so fully affirms the local context that the gospel is reduced to a cultural framework; we might therefore lose self-critical awareness, either by superficial romanticizing or by opening ourselves up to relativism. As we engage, we must be critical of our own ethnocultural context to comprehend the limits of our theological view and the ways this view may be misinformed by existing oppressive ideologies.

The praxis model also perceives the two theological sources – scripture and Christian tradition – as culturally conditioned, but it believes that God is still working among people, especially people who are oppressed and experience poverty and marginalization. It is up to Christians to discern the "signs of the times." One's particular context is usually good and trustworthy, but it is prone to distortion by way of existing oppressive ideologies, norms, and values. Therefore, one needs to examine scripture and Christian tradition with a critical lens as resources to direct social change. This model does not simply seek a culturally and socially relevant Christian message, it also commits to Christian action and justice as linked to the prophetic teachings in the Hebrew Bible and the books of the Gospel. Through this praxis of action and reflection, one develops a theology that is genuinely relevant to one's context. One of the critiques of this model receives is that it has a close connection with Marxism.

The fourth model, the synthetic model, emphasizes dialogue, openness, and pluralism, and it takes a "both/and" attitude. It aims to synthesize the best elements from the previous three models. It recognizes that the context, scripture, and Christian tradition are all limited, and so all three of them need to be constantly in dialogue to find a middle ground. However, this model risks becoming "wishy-washy" by failing to be faithful either to Christian tradition or to the concerns and problems of various ethnocultural contexts. Also, by emphasizing the importance of dialogue, the interaction between two local contexts can be taken over and manipulated by a dominant culture and/or dialogue partners.

The starting point of theology for the transcendental or subjective model is one's "own religious experience and one's own experience of oneself,"[37] rather than how Christian faith can be authentically expressed in a particular context. It focuses more on the self who is reflecting than on the content of the reflection. This approach demonstrates that one's experience is closely tied to the wider experience of humanity; what one personally experiences is similar to what one's community, and indeed all humanity, have experienced in every culture throughout human history. Consequently, the objective of this model is not to find an appropriate theological articulation of the gospel, but, rather, to search for one's authentic subjectivity – "authenticity as a believer, and authenticity as a person in a very specific cultural and historical context."[38] The gospel is not "out there"; rather, it is revealed to the person who listens to their personal experience and social location and who learns about God through various theological sources. While it is a fresh approach to theology, and a deeply philosophical one at that, it is sometimes critiqued for being too abstract and ideal. Further, the universality that this approach asserts is a false universality, in that too little attention is given to cultural/contextual formation.

The sixth model is countercultural, and as Bevans has noted, Anabaptist theologies, especially the messianic community and the missional church, fall into this model. This model emphasizes God's truth as revealed through Jesus Christ, and it points to Christians as the ones who live out this gospel of Jesus. It is not anti-cultural per se, but it views several cultural elements as standing against the gospel, such as distorted myths and oppressive practices. These elements should be aligned to the gospel. Hence, the church is called to not conform to the world but to instead be a missional church to the world. Like the praxis model, this model is committed to social change, but it also adopts a hermeneutic of suspicion of one's context in light of the gospel criteria. Although this model invites a strong engagement with context, the countercultural approach can easily assume an anti-cultural guise and therefore belittle or even demonize others' cultural practices. Also, this model is in danger of sliding into sectarianism and exclusivism by arguing that some churches in this model have theologically and biblically correct views, while others do not; these churches might then withdraw from engagement with other church traditions.[39]

After presenting these six models, Bevans clarifies that all models are valid in some ways, and none can claim hegemony. Each has distinct advantages, as well as some points of weakness; there is no need to adhere to only one model. Further, depending where one is situated, a person can choose one model for a particular circumstance or period of time. For instance, when one is living in an environment that requires radical social change, one might prefer the praxis model rather than the translation model. Or, in a situation in which one is sharing the gospel in a foreign country, one might prefer the translation model instead of the countercultural model.[40]

In the Canadian context, where white supremacy and settler colonialism are prevalent, I argue that Mennonites should strive for an integration of the anthropological, praxis, and countercultural models. A robust and broadly conceived liberative theology captures this integration well. As observed in the definition of culture introduced above, views of God, truth, and the world are culturally conditioned. Consequently, one's interpretation of the Bible and Christian tradition is deeply shaped by one's ethnocultural context. This fundamental insight is reflected in the anthropological model. However, cultures have been shaped by colonialism, nationalism, other ideologies and hegemonic power asymmetries, and so instead of accepting a wholesale cultural romanticism, Christians should adopt a critical perspective toward the cultures and social structures that surround them. Moreover, since their understanding of the Bible and tradition is interpreted through a cultural lens, Christians also need to be aware of the limits and potential failures of their interpretations and maintain a suspicion about claiming too much. This requires a continuous cycle of praxis, analysis, and reflection in which one critically sees one's context; discerns how God is working in that context through various theological sources like the Bible, traditions, social science, and others; and acts to bring about social transformation. In this sense, the praxis model has much to offer. This approach is not foreign to Mennonites since standing against Christendom is part of Mennonite tradition. As Christians critically analyze the surrounding cultural context in light of the gospel, they should offer an alternative vision. Based on scripture and Christian tradition, Christians are to offer an alternative and life-giving vision and way of life. Thus, there is much to commend in the countercultural model, which resonates with Mennonite perspectives because striving to be an alternative and contrasting community in the world is core to the Mennonites' beliefs of ecclesiology, mission, and discipleship.

By combining these three models, the strengths of each helps to avoid the potential weaknesses of any one model. Reducing the gospel to a cultural framework and lacking self-critical awareness are potential dangers of the anthropological model, but the praxis and the countercultural models invite critical examination of one's ethnocultural context, faith, and beliefs, and they urge us to hold on to the gospel presented by Jesus. Although the praxis model is critiqued for having a close connection with Marxism, when this model is aligned and joined with the countercultural model, Marxist theories and criticisms can be used as tools based on the gospel criteria to name and unmask oppressive practices in society, without being part of a larger Marxist agenda. Furthermore, the anthropological and the praxis models can challenge the countercultural model not to be anti-cultural, sectarian, or exclusionary, and they guide us toward a more active participation in social transformation.

As I maintain the tensions among these three models, I propose a liberative approach that is based on the norms of justice and love, a striving toward transformation and a holistic well-being for all of God's creation. This approach seeks "total liberation," which Gorringe describes as the "release from injustice, oppression and poverty, but also, and only through, [the] release from inner compulsions, patterns of violence, patterns of domination, and ultimately death."[41] Another name he gives to this total liberation is "shalom."[42] While this liberative approach may be seen as a kind of synthetic model, I distance myself from it for two reasons. First, even though I recognize that the synthetic approach strives to integrate the three different models, my approach does not fit Bevans's description of the synthetic model. Specifically, his description of the synthetic model combines the translation, anthropological, and praxis models but not the countercultural model. Furthermore, my approach emphasizes personal, communal, and social transformation, which is not the main focus of the synthetic model. I seek to highlight the intersecting strengths of the three models.

To reiterate, our faith and theology are deeply influenced but not reducible to our ethnocultural context. The gospel criteria of justice and liberation offer a critical principles that stop contexts from collapsing on themselves. Still, our ethnocultural context is influenced by ideologies and oppressive practices. This does not mean that cultures are completely distorted and are all wrong and evil. Indeed, there are positive and insightful understandings of life, God, our world embedded in various cultural frameworks. These theological views are rooted in the doctrine of Creation, and they are resources that become evident and empowering in relationship to the gospel. They can be used for resisting oppression as well as forming alternative cultures. For this reason, through a liberative theological perspective, Christians may be better able to deconstruct and reconstruct their Christian faith and practices as they critically examine all dimensions of their lives.

As this intercultural theological project is based in Canada, its contextual nature compels a closer examination and assessment of the Canadian context. Because this book cannot explore all aspects of the Canadian cultural context, it focuses specifically on how difference is engaged. Thus, I will examine Canadian multiculturalism as a dominant way of framing difference in the public square, noting how difference is managed and controlled through white supremacism and settler colonialism. Such an examination will help show not only how cultural, ethnic, and racial diversity are understood from the government standpoint, but also how marginalized social groups are socially, politically, and economically excluded under the guise of "multiculturalism." A social group is a group of people who are interconnected with one another because of their similar lifestyle or social practices, and they are differentiated from other groups according to these cultural forms.

4

Canadian Multiculturalism and Interculturality

In an article for *Douglas Magazine*, Ruth Mojeed, a Nigerian Canadian woman, shared her experience living in Canadian multicultural society. She highlights such issues as police brutality predominantly affecting Indigenous and racialized people and reflecting deeper systemic discrimination. Mojeed points out that the veneer of politeness that often prevails in Canadian society masks ongoing inequality and discrimination in workplaces and in everyday social interactions. The expectation that newcomers should have "Canadian experience" acts as a barrier, preventing qualified immigrants from securing jobs. She criticizes the superficial appreciation of cultural diversity, in which cultural artifacts like food are valued more than the stories and efforts behind them. Additionally, Indigenous and racialized youth face significant disparities compared to their white counterparts when it comes to accessing economic and social opportunities.

Mojeed shares her personal challenges "As a young woman of colour with some measure of privilege – education, language (not forgetting the Nigerian accent), and relative socio-economic comfort," explaining that she has "also been on the short end of the privilege yardstick. I have had to deal with assumptions and prejudices that are often left unspoken about my capabilities, intellect (or lack thereof) when stereotypes become the true talebearer and unconscious biases are acted upon. I have had to share my perspectives over and over without any recourse to action, until it came in from a more familiar source, often the person with the right accent, local experience, and skin colour. And there is the issue of intersectionality: Black people, like any other group, must deal with layers of issues including religion, age, gender, etc."[1]

She calls out the lack of representation and policy support for BIPOC communities in government and leadership roles, as well as the commonplace experience of racial profiling in stores, which she says underscores the pervasive nature of racism in Canada. Mojeed urges people to acknowledge and "PLEASE SEE COLOUR," as it encompasses the rich histories and struggles of generations of immigrants and racialized people. She believes that understanding and sharing these experiences is crucial if we are to move beyond our superficial differences and fostering genuine inclusivity and understanding.[2]

One dominant approach for dealing with cultural, ethnic, and racial difference in Canada is Canadian multiculturalism, an approach with its own history and agenda that, broadly conceived, aims at arranging and organizing difference according to the purpose of the government. To counter biculturalism, in 1971 Prime Minister Pierre Trudeau's government introduced its multiculturalism policy, while maintaining English and French as Canada's official languages. Later, through the Constitution Act (1982) and the Canadian Charter of Rights and Freedoms, multiculturalism was enshrined in law as a unique characteristic of Canadian society. In 1988, the government passed the Multiculturalism Act, and through this, Canada became the first nation to "give legal weight to multiculturalism."[3] The central idea of the act is to "promote the full and equitable participation of individuals and communities of all origins in the continuing evolution and shaping of all aspects of Canadian society and assist them in the elimination of any barrier to that participation."[4] The act asserts that the government takes seriously the ethnic diversity that exists within the country, seeks to recognize each ethnic community, and fosters the rich multicultural character of Canadian society. With the passing of this act, all federal institutions were required to play an active leadership role in promoting multiculturalism.

Canadian multiculturalism is more than just state policy, however, it is also an ideology that profoundly shapes the socio-political and economic realities of all Canadians living together in this nation-state. The Canadian Multiculturalism Act declares that "multiculturalism is a fundamental characteristic of the Canadian heritage and identity."[5] This statement asserts that multiculturalism is the "master narrative of the nation,"[6] even influencing how Canadians think about themselves in relation to other countries. This form of multiculturalism emerged from a specific time and was constructed for a particular goal and purpose. For this reason, it is crucial to understand and critically examine Canadian multiculturalism if we are to truly comprehend the Canadian context.

In critically analyzing Canadian multiculturalism, it is helpful to understand three concepts in particular: oppression, racism, and settler colonialism. Since racism has already been covered in the previous chapter, let us first turn to the two other terms before we hear what critical social theorists have to say about Canadian multiculturalism. My understanding of oppression is informed by Iris Marion Young, who explains that oppression is in a sense structural rather than the result of individual choices. The causes of oppression are embedded in unquestioned norms, habits, symbols, and underlying institutional rules. In this sense, "oppression" refers to the vast and deep injustices some social groups "suffer as a consequence of often unconscious assumptions and reactions of well-meaning people in ordinary interactions, media and cultural stereotypes, and structural features of bureaucratic hierarchies and market mechanisms – in short, the normal processes of everyday life."[7] Marion Young also explains that in Western society, five types of oppression can be identified: exploitation, marginalization, powerlessness, cultural imperialism, and systemic violence. Briefly stated, exploitation is a steady process wherein the labour of a particular social group is transferred to benefit another group or groups. This process not only create inequalities in the distribution of goods and services but also takes away opportunities to create affective relationships between different social groups. Marginalization means expelling a social group from participation in social goods and communal life, and, taken to an extreme, it can even result in extermination. Powerlessness is when one's agency and power is taken away, and others come to make decisions for them. Cultural imperialism is not only the universalization of a dominant group's culture but also the instantiation of that culture as a hegemonic norm and the ideal way of life of a society, while the rest are dismissed. Those who are outside or do not belong to this norm are seen as inferior. An oppressed person might also internalize this view. Systemic violence is a violence directed at members of certain social groups simply because they belong to those groups. While it might seem that random violence is directed at individual people, in a larger perspective, one can observe that violence is done frequently to certain social groups.[8]

Settler colonialism is a particular type of colonialism where the colonizers replace the existing Indigenous people and systems and claim sovereignty over the land in order to inhabit it permanently. Because the colonizers seek to occupy the space permanently, their end goal is to exterminate and/or to force Indigenous people to assimilate to the colonial society and its false national narratives so that they do not challenge white settlers. In this context, the term "reconciliation" has been used as a colonial tool to pressure Indigenous people to let go of past injustices and focus on how to live "peacefully" under the white settlers' colonial structure and system. In similar way, Canadian multiculturalism has also been used by the government to advance the agenda of settler colonialism and to hide the racism and the five types of oppression that people of colour experience in Canada. These themes will be examined in more detail with reference to the work of Canadian social theorists like Himani Bannerji, Carl James, Augie Fleras, and Jean Leonard Elliott.

The Multiculturalism Act portrays Canadian society as an inclusive and diverse polity that strives to give equal opportunity and treatment to each individual, without demanding that people surrender their religious and cultural values. Nonetheless, there is a contravening undertow that threatens to undo these positive aims. This dynamic is vividly illustrated through the real-life experiences of Ruth Mojeed, whose story was shared at the outset of this chapter. Critical social theorists condemn Canadian multiculturalism for its racist, oppressive, and assimilationist elements. Himani Bannerji contends that Trudeau adopted multiculturalism as official policy out of political interests rather than concern for social justice. During the late 1960s and the early 1970s, a rivalry was growing between the Canadian federal government and francophone Canadians; people in Quebec sought to be independent from the Canadian government. At the same time, there was a rapid influx of immigrants from the Global South, and the demand for justice and rights for Indigenous communities was increasing. In order to defuse this rivalry, to organize and control immigration, and to silence the demand for Indigenous rights, Trudeau adopted the policy of multiculturalism.[9] Even though the policy was written with inclusive language, it was clearly an attempt to manage diversity and control public discourse rather than bring about a robust inclusion of differences. Further, Canadian multiculturalism is state multiculturalism – it is initiated, organized, and promoted by the government – rather than emerging from the grassroots. As a consequence, this concept of multiculturalism contains the agendas and the ideological concerns of the government, which exerts a profound degree of control over the socio-cultural and legal-economic affairs of Canadians.

Since the people with power in Canadian society are predominantly of European descent, multiculturalism is used as a strategy to assimilate and tolerate racialized and minoritized people and Indigenous communities rather than to genuinely support them. Canadian multiculturalism exists within a bilingual framework and claims that there is no one official culture or favoured ethnic group. However, as Carl James observes, this actually reinforces the British and French ethno-cultural identities and promotes assimilation "under the guise of integration of 'other ethnic groups' and while alluding to 'the undisputable role played by Canadians of French and British origin.'"[10] Along the same line, Fleras and Elliott add that multiculturalism was used for several ends: to weaken oppositional groups by reshaping official policy; to force groups to compete with each other within the multicultural framework; to appeal to popular sentiments and public instincts and receive wider public support; to create the appearance of change (as opposed to actual change); to modify the interests of minority groups so that the government could better control and manage them; and to secure the goodwill and admiration of the international community by presenting Canada as a welcoming and inclusive nation.[11]

Additionally, Canadian multiculturalism has been criticized because, implicitly and explicitly, it seeks to obscure the histories of oppression and injustice experienced by Indigenous people, people of colour, and ethnic minority groups. By focusing on "celebrating diversity," colonialism, racism, white privilege, sexism, patriarchy, and heteronormativity are downplayed. By espousing multiculturalism, one may be perceived as correcting the racist history of Canada and pretending that such inequities do not exist in the present. It also focuses the attention on the "tolerant" character of contemporary Canadian society and the good intention of welcoming other peoples. In so doing, the policy of multiculturalism operates as a smokescreen that hides the experiences of racialized and minoritized peoples in Canada today. Consequently, as Dhamoon writes, multiculturalism "does not name the oppressors or require that the land of multicultural Canada be given back to [I]ndigenous people; nor does it directly attend to the problems of violence, unemployment, and poverty ... And it does not acknowledge the ways in which people of colour and [I]ndigenous people resist white patriarchal capitalist hegemony."[12] Similarly, Bannerji asserts that the multicultural mosaic masks the histories of conquest, war, and exclusion, the dark side of the nation.[13] Through this masking, various types of oppression and injustice remain unexamined. For this reason, it is not enough to merely *acknowledge* diversity in Canada. Multiculturalism constructs an artificial idea of difference that can be managed and implicitly assimilated, despite its ostensible aim to include. Hence, even the more recent language of "integration" can be problematic and assimilative in its thrust. What is required, as Fleras and Elliott argue, is that we confront the broader social and political forces that construct "diversity" and "consider who decides what diversity means, and what their motives are ... What is needed instead is an approach that defines diversity as a function of power relations in society."[14] For this reason, we must scrutinize the power dynamics of Canadian multiculturalism for the ways in which it is used to manage and control diversity.

Another criticism directed at the policy of multiculturalism pertains to its overemphasis of a very limited understanding of culture and cultural groups. In a more comprehensive understanding of culture, diverse marker of identity like ethnicity, race, and gender are interconnected. Yet, from the perspective of multicultural policy, the understanding of culture is limited to a simplistic and monolithic view of people's peculiar cultural traditions as expressed through food, rituals, customs, and cultural group identity (as uniform throughout, lacking diversity and fluidity). In this sense, critical scrutiny is deflected away from issues of power inequity and race, gender, sexuality, disability, and so on, assuming that all the people in the same cultural group believe and act somewhat similarly. This has the net effect of reinforcing existing stereotypes. Several critical social theorists identify multiculturalism as problematic because of this unidimensional understanding of difference. This is why, as Kimberlé Crenshaw advocates, it is crucial to maintain an understanding of intersectionality.[15] Intersectionality allows us to recognize the complex oppressions that exist in a multicultural society, highlights how oppression is multivalent and multi-dimensional, and offers a critical vantage point on multiculturalism. Recognition and tolerance of cultural differences will not adequately address the various forms of oppression – ranging from economic and social to political – that cultural groups experience.

Based on the criticisms stated above, in a nutshell, Canadian multiculturalism serves white European settlers in positions of political and socio-economic power. As a result, several social groups are oppressed via such a policy. For instance, Canadian multiculturalism treats Indigenous peoples as just one of many cultural and ethnic groups. This classification co-opts these communities into a settler-colonial framework, treating them as equivalent to other minority groups. Consequently, it overlooks the historical injustices committed by white settlers, dismisses Indigenous people's territorial claims to sovereignty, and ignores their unique concerns such as recovering their land, resisting ongoing colonial structures, and regaining their own sovereign systems of governance.

Since whiteness is the norm within this vision of multiculturalism, the policy also oppresses when it is utilized to consume and to control non-whites. Differences in economic and political outcomes occur not simply because ethnic groups do not get enough cultural recognition, but also because they are not given enough political and economic support and opportunities. These aspects are ignored because multiculturalism views difference as something to tolerate rather than the result of racism and white supremacy. Hogarth and Fletcher show that one of the reasons why immigrants and Indigenous people are grossly underemployed is because of the "unwillingness of Canadian employers to accept anything that is not 'Canadian,' including language, accent, education, and color."[16] Ironically, here "Canadian" refers to white settlers of European descent. Thus, the partial "respect" accorded non-white cultures is not a true respect; it does not extend to critical areas such as equal employment opportunities, political representation, access to quality education, and fair treatment within the legal system. Consequently, the rhetoric of respect is merely a facade.

Through multiculturalism, racialized women are also oppressed. In the policy and activities of multiculturalism, culture is understood as rigid, traditional, and uniform. Therefore, as multiculturalism supports different cultures, it inadvertently blesses oppressive "cultural" values and practices that are patriarchal, homophobic, and xenophobic. This issue is illustrated quite well in the famous debate that Susan Moller

Okin, a political theorist, initiated by asking scholars from the United States, Canada, and United Kingdom a simple question: Is multiculturalism bad for women?[17]

To reiterate, Canadian multiculturalism was not created in a vacuum. It was created on the land that was unjustly taken from Indigenous people by white settlers; these settlers were interested in maintaining their power and the status quo in a context characterized by a growing influx of immigrant communities. From its beginning, Canadian multiculturalism has been state multiculturalism; the government has been actively involved in shaping, managing, and promoting it. Thus, multiculturalism is interconnected with settler colonialism, white supremacy, racism, and capitalism. Even though the Multiculturalism Act encourages different ethnic groups to engage in various cultural activities (e.g., learn other languages, customs, rituals, and cultural practices), it does not provide the necessary economic resources and power for these groups to confront systemic racism and to be actively involved in key questions. Ethnic minorities are not given enough opportunities and spaces to shape the future of Canadian law and policy, or to access political and economic resources. For genuine social transformation, a fair distribution of economic resources and power is required. And from the perspective of Indigenous communities, there should be a fair sharing of the land, a mending of the treaties broken by the white settlers, and a system of sovereign Indigenous governance.

Foregrounding the limits of Canadian multiculturalism, several alternative approaches have emerged for the Canadian context. An in-depth evaluation of each of these approaches is beyond the scope of this book, but they merit brief consideration here, as they represent efforts to better engage with diverse social groups, especially marginalized groups. The first approach is espoused by critical social theorists like Sneja Gunew, Hogarth, and Fletcher, who advocate for a *critical multiculturalism*. Gunew argues that multiculturalism needs to be tied with anti-racism and must consider the cultural, economic, and political aspects of visible minorities, as well as the wider legacy of colonialism in Canada.[18] Hogarth and Fletcher press for a better understanding of power inequalities among different groups, and for the integration of anti-racism and social justice; they note that critical multiculturalism must be willing to seek structural change.[19] Although Bannerji does not argue for critical multiculturalism, she contends that the possibilities for constructing a radically different social structure are only apparent from the vantage point of those who have been "othered." By listening more attentively to these perspectives, society can create a better place for all.[20] This position leans toward Lowman and Barker's claim that decolonizing work can only be done in concert by settlers and Indigenous people.[21]

Another approach that has emerged is *interculturalism*. Criticizing multiculturalism as being centred around Canadian anglophones and for not going far enough to integrate various social groups, the Quebec government has adopted a policy of interculturalism, which promotes cultural exchanges among different cultural groups in an effort to avoid the formation of ethnic enclaves. This policy recognizes the cultural diversity within Quebec and, instead of simply tolerating the differences among social groups, it seeks an active dialogue between them – for the purpose of integrating or fusing differences into a common and shared public life within a francophone framework. Different from federal multiculturalism, Quebec is pursuing "convergence" through the policy of interculturalism.[22] Some researchers, such as Dimitrios Karmis, claim that interculturalism is the most advanced form of pluralism that currently exists. Karmis claim rests on three assertions. First, that interculturalism is more encompassing than multiculturalism because it is not limited to cultural groups but is also open to other subcultures and lifestyles, like gay culture. Second, instead of juxtaposing different cultural communities, it seeks to integrate them. Third, it acknowledges that people have multiple identities, and so no one identity factor should dominate any others.[23] However, it should be noted that in Quebec this "convergence" and "integration" must happen within the francophone framework, which amounts to an affirmation of the dominant position of francophone culture and language. In other words, any "reasonable accommodation" carries an assimilative logic, wherein power still resides in the dominant culture, which in this case is the francophone culture. Consequently, this leads toward a practice of cultural imperialism, in which racialized ethnic groups are required to accept francophone culture as the official, public culture, and their own cultures as merely private forms of expression.

Attempts to grapple with difference in Canada have occurred not only at a societal level but also at an organizational level. In the midst of a growing awareness of diversity, noticing rising numbers of incoming immigrants and refugees in Canada, and observing the limited understanding of multiculturalism expressed by government officials, several denominations have begun to explore what it means for the church to live faithfully and to witness actively in such a social and political context. As a result, several church organizations have committed to striving toward interculturality in church and ministry. For instance, Tyndale University established the Tyndale Intercultural Ministries Centre in 1998 to train current and future church leaders for intercultural ministries, although the centre's perception of interculturality tends to emphasize cross-cultural ministry, a way to evangelize people from other cultural traditions.[24] In 2006, the United Church of Canada purposefully chose to be an intercultural church,[25] and in 2011, the Anglican Church of Canada's Toronto diocese stated its intention to become an intercultural church.[26] Moreover, in 2017, the Canadian Churches' Forum for Global Ministries changed its name to the Forum for Intercultural Leadership and Learning and began to offer training and programs to help Canadian churches to become intercultural, especially to the denominations connected through the Canadian Council of Churches.[27] The above organizations all made an intentional shift toward the work of interculturality, regardless of their perhaps diverging understandings of that concept. Although MC Canada has not officially committed to being an intercultural church, there is certainly a growing interest among its members in becoming one, and several discussions are happening at the leadership level. For instance, in March 2020, Mennonite Church Eastern Canada appointed and hired Fanosie Legesse to serve as intercultural mission minister, a new position. Another good example came in February 2021, when MC Canada formed an Intercultural Church Steering Committee to provide leadership to the national and regional churches as the denomination seeks to become an intercultural church.

Summarizing the critiques of Canadian multiculturalism and discussions of various alternatives, it is clear that the government's current approach to grappling with diverse social groups is harmful and oppressive to racialized communities. The critical multiculturalism proposed by some social theorists seems to be most promising, but that is a discussion for a different book. Since this book is about how Mennonite churches can live faithfully in Canadian multicultural society, I will focus on the alternative approach, which entails working toward the construction of an intercultural church. Yet, integrating the insights of critical social theorists, I argue that Mennonites, rather than seeking to be just *any* kind of intercultural church, should instead work to become a *decolonizing and anti-racist* community that centres the lived experiences of marginalized people and communities. Recognizing that the term "intercultural" may be a foreign concept for some, before examining how MC Canada can become a critical intercultural church, I first offer a closer examination of the concept of interculturality.

Features of Intercultural Living and Dialogue

In a community or society composed of individuals from various ethnocultural, religious, and socio-economic backgrounds, people have to negotiate difference. Difference can be treated positively or negatively. Most commonly, it is viewed negatively because it is perceived as a threat to the status quo and the dominant group's agreed characteristics, values, and norms, which create a sense of commonality or sameness among them. Theologian and missiologist Robert Schreiter explains that throughout humanity's encounters with difference in history, we can identify at least five strategic postures that do not respect difference and that try to collapse what is perceived as "other" into the dominant culture and world view, or even to exclude it altogether. The first strategy is to homogenize the other by ignoring or downplaying the differences that exist between people, so that the other is perceived as little different from oneself. This method pressures the other to conform and to assimilate to the dominant group. If the other does not conform, the dominant people categorize them as the source of trouble and disunity. The second strategy is to colonize the other by including them coercively through direct or indirect means. Often, education and religion are used to "fix" or "erase" difference. The third strategy demonizes the other by believing that the difference they exhibit is so extreme as to threaten a sense of communal unity, thereby warranting the other's exclusion. Usually, the dominant group is considered normal and neutral, while the other is considered deviant. The dominant group is essentializing or absolutizing that difference. The fourth strategy romanticizes the other, who is seen as unique and superior in its otherness, without this otherness being seen as a threat to the dominant group. Although no active coercion is involved in this method, it is still a form of colonializing because the other often bears the projection of ideals from the dominant group's imagination. Idealizing is a form of colonizing. The fifth strategy is pluralizing the other by believing that difference does not matter because we are all different. This approach is actually tantamount to denial, and it seeks in effect to homogenize the other.[28] As an alternative to these five strategies, genuine intercultural relationships and community seek to respect differences while trying neither to collapse nor exclude the other.

As one learns more about interculturality, one will realize that it involves different discourses. The term is being utilized by scholars from several fields of study, including education, communication studies, philosophy, missiology, and theology. Even among these scholars, there are variations in how they interpret interculturality, what resources they use to explain it, and why they choose the word. Despite these distinctions, certain key concepts and ideas are often employed to explicate interculturality. For the purposes of this study, I draw from the work of Anthony Gittins and Olga Consuelo Vélez Caro, because they correspond to Mennonite perspectives that inform the approach taken in chapter 5, and because they offer a theoretical framing of what interculturality means theo-ethically. After examining their understanding of interculturality, I offer my own working "definition" of the term.[29]

Gittins, a theologian examining interculturality through a postmodern anthropological lens, offers a nuanced understanding of interculturality. Firstly, he underscores that it is a deliberate, faith-driven endeavour. It arises from the recognition that faith is inherently intertwined with culture. When individuals from diverse cultural backgrounds come together, they may face challenges, but these challenges should not be seen as problems to be fixed. Instead, intercultural living is a complex and non-natural process that cannot be reduced to a set of techniques. Despite its difficulty, Gittins suggests that it is a goal aligned with God's intentions and an essential step toward fostering societies where no single cultural group dominates. Achieving interculturality demands more than just good intentions and goodwill; it requires commitment, sustained effort, skill, and virtuous qualities. Ultimately, it thrives on diplomacy, compromise, dialogue, and a shared vision that inspires collective effort and provides the necessary means to sustain it.[30] In essence, Gittins portrays interculturality as a multi-faceted, faith-driven journey that transcends simplistic solutions.

As these descriptions affirm, interculturality is a faith-based endeavour that requires intentionality and commitment from all ethnocultural groups because every member must work to find new ways of relating, communicating, and living. As people move away from their own cultural group (their comfort zone) to engage with diverse others, they must find alternative ways of being Christians together in humility – by listening to one another, shaping and influencing one another, and jointly building a society where everyone can belong, and where no one needs to assimilate to the dominant group or culture. Interculturality is not an easy task, but it is work that we Christians are called to do if we truly believe in the unity in Christ, in which no member is excluded and everyone is fully welcomed, respected, and honoured.

Caro, a Colombian feminist theologian, offers a comprehensive view of interculturality that underscores its dynamic essence. She describes it as a journey into uncharted territory whereby individuals from diverse cultural backgrounds collaborate to create something new, seeking common ground while rejecting elements of dominance or colonization. In this process, they aim to establish an inclusive space where every voice is heard, challenging their own cultural biases and judgments in the process. Embracing interculturality begins with recognizing human limitations and the need to let go of the impulse to absolutize or sacralize one's own culture in favour of embracing change. Participants adopt a humble attitude, constantly questioning their interpretations of reality and remaining open to the possibility that others may have a more accurate perspective. While interculturality involves starting from one's cultural tradition, rather than ensuring that one remain fixed in that position, it serves as a bridge by which one might connect with others, emphasizing the fluid and dynamic nature of cultural interaction.[31] Caro echoes some of the points made by Gittins, but she offers a deeper understanding of intercultural work and, mindful of the power dynamics within these relationships, notes that each person brings certain prejudices, and that we all have the tendency to colonize and dominate others. Therefore, critical thinking is essential in intercultural endeavour.

The perspectives offered by these two theologians are quite helpful because they depict clearly and carefully what interculturality entails, how to include all voices, and what dangers to avoid. Nonetheless, since this book specifically focuses on the work of becoming an intercultural community of faith, for our purposes their points pertain too specifically to the individual level, and they do not go far enough in examining how churches can become intercultural. My contribution to the discourse of interculturality in the discipline of theology aims to do two things: (1) interrogate more fully why Mennonites (and Christian churches in general) need to be intercultural in the Canadian context; and (2) present how this may be possible from an explicitly Anabaptist-Mennonite perspective.

Based broadly on the these two scholars' descriptions of interculturality, my own working definition of interculturality can be stated as follows: an active respectful interaction among different cultural groups to enrich one another by sharing aspects of their cultures while seeking mutual relationship and a fair distribution of power among all groups in order to create a more loving, just, and peaceful community and society where no group tries to dominate and colonize any other. Although intercultural engagement is challenging because it entails intentional work to find alternative ways of living, relating, and thinking, it is possible.

Nevertheless, to have this just, respectful, and mutual interaction among different cultural groups in Canada, where settler colonialism and white supremacy are embedded in the nation's history, formation, and current socio-economic system and policies, church communities need to be decolonial and anti-racist. To be a decolonial church is to be deeply aware of the history of colonization and the harm it has caused and continues to cause primarily to Indigenous people but also to all settlers, both white and people of colour, in Canada. It also means to unlearn the colonial epistemology and lifestyle, resisting any system and policies that seek to assimilate Indigenous people, re-centring and restoring Indigenous communities, and finding new ways to live together. The journey of decolonization will be different for white settlers, Indigenous people, and racialized people, but everyone who lives and interacts in Canada is called to be part of this long journey.

To assume the work of decolonizing is to be anti-racist, because settler colonialism utilizes systemic racism to discriminate against non-whites. In a society that embraces white supremacy and perpetuates racism, there is no neutral stance; in other words, one cannot be merely non-racist. To remain silent and do nothing in the face of systemic racism is to allow oneself to be complicit with it. Hence, in Canada, one is either racist or anti-racist. To be an anti-racist church means to actively identify and eliminate individual, institutional, and systemic racism. It means transforming the church's beliefs, values, organizational structures, policies, and practices and attitudes so that power and resources are more equitably shared among white and racialized people. The end goal of this endeavour is to strive toward God's shalom through racial justice and collective healing.

Some examples of anti-racist practices include recognizing that we are all impacted by racism and that we all have differences in our lived experiences; being aware of our own individual biases and complicity in racism and continually learning the history of racism and anti-racism movements in Canada; and actively confronting and overturning existing barriers faced by racialized people (e.g., barriers to employment, resources, policies, and procedures within institutions). Particularly for whites, they can engage in learning how white privilege shows up in one's life and address internalized racial superiority/white supremacy. As part of kenotic practices, they can use their white privilege to be an "upstander" – someone who interrupts racism when they see it and actively provides space and opportunities for racialized people to be empowered and flourish in a non-patronizing manner. For BIPOC, anti-racist practices can include celebrating the beauty and value of one's race and cultural identities as image bearers of God, working to heal one's trauma and build anti-racist resilience, and addressing internalized feelings of racial inferiority and the pressure to fulfil stereotypical notions of the "model minority." At the same time, it is important to recognize that all racial groups are struggling in some way under white supremacy. Misinformation, prejudice, and harm can exist between people of colour, and these, too, need to be confronted. This entails knowing how histories of colonization, enslavement, and immigration impact particular groups. In turn, this means recognizing the intersectional oppression experienced by different people of colour.

An Anabaptist-Mennonite Perspective on Interculturality: Shalom

As a way to develop an Anabaptist-Mennonite perspective on interculturality, I propose shalom as a foundational principle. I intentionally choose the term "shalom" instead of "peace" because I agree with Duane Friesen and Malinda Berry that the latter term has been used in a limited way that mostly focuses on the personal level. However, because the traditional Anabaptist-Mennonite understanding of shalom lacks an emphasis on interculturality, I incorporate the notion of *convivencia* to deepen and expand its meaning.

When theologians and philosophers write about interculturality, they repeatedly use the word *convivencia*, a Spanish word that means "living together-ness." The term has been utilized in the field of mission studies, and the first person to introduce it to missiology was Theo Sundermeier, a Heidelberg scholar in missiology and religious studies.[32] As he reflected on what he had experienced during his time in Africa, he adopted the term from liberation theology to express his experience and how *convivencia* helps reimagine mission. For him, this means learning from one another, helping one another, and celebrating with one another in community.[33] It is a "basic dimension of human community that transcends one's own circles (one's own family group, ethnic group, group of friends, or one's own milieu) – not in the sense of fusing people together but rather of helping them live together by sharing a common interest in humanity."[34]

As Sundermeier indicates, *convivencia* is a term used widely to describe the life of base ecclesial communities in Latin America. In this light, Leonardo Boff describes *convivencia* as living with others and sharing dynamically in others' lives, ways of being, struggles, quests, defeats, and victories. Such co-living welcomes difference, rather than existing in spite of it. Moreover, *convivencia* occurs when "differences are relativized in favor of common points, and this allows for the rise of necessary converging that forms the concrete basis for a peaceful co-living, despite the continued existence of some levels of tension due to genuine difference."[35] In other words, co-living happens when people embrace the tension between respecting their differences and not essentializing or absolutizing them. Living in this tension, people strive toward peaceful co-living for all as they mutually create new forms of relationship and ways of life. In this peaceful co-living, our relationship with the environment is also crucial because humans only have one planet. Without caring for our "home," there cannot be co-living because the lives of all living beings will be at stake.

Convivencia is also used by Raul Fornet-Betancourt, a Cuban philosopher who resides in Germany and teaches intercultural philosophy and theology. Like Sundermeier and Boff, Fornet-Betancourt describes *convivencia* as an intentional effort to live together in solidarity with those who are different.[36] Yet, going beyond the interpretations put forth by Sundermeier and Boff, Fornet-Betancourt asserts that for *convivencia* to be sustainable, the order of the current world needs to shift so that it becomes a place of relationship and mutual support, in which people bring their traditions to enhance co-living, eliminating any type of alienation and oppression, such as ethnocentrism, racism, traditionalism, culturalism, elitism, institutionalism, capitalism, and militarism. Stated differently, while each person is required to work and journey together toward *convivencia*, particular systems and structures need to be created to sustain and enhance it. Therefore, for Fornet-Betancourt, *convivencia* is also an alternative political-cultural project that seeks to transform power asymmetries and the relationship between domination and subordination that are rooted in our culture and society, so that marginalized social groups can live with full dignity and thrive.[37] *Convivencia* seeks to do this by creating more just conditions and environments where people from all ethnocultural groups feel that they have their own space and resources, and where these groups are empowered to have genuine interaction with each other.[38]

From an Anabaptist perspective, the *convivencia* Fornet-Betancourt describes deeply resonates with the biblical notion of shalom. A renowned Mennonite Old Testament scholar, Perry Yoder, asserts that "shalom" is the biblical word for salvation, justice, and peace. He explains that it has three shades of meaning. The first, and the one that is used most often in the Hebrew Bible, is "marked by the presence of [a] physical state of well-being and by the absence of physical threats like war, disease, and famine."[39] In this aspect, it is crucial that all people have their physical needs met. The second shade of shalom refers to social relationships, right relationship, and respect among people within a society and community. The third is the "presence of integrity and straightforwardness, the opposite of deceit."[40] This aspect focuses more on morality. After explaining these aspects of shalom, Yoder states that they are interconnected, and that there is no shalom if one's physical needs are not met, injustice and oppression exist, or moral integrity and well-being are absent. It is only when all of these aspects are realized that there is shalom.[41] Yoder further argues that justice is the basis for shalom. Shalom seeks liberation for everyone who is caught in any kind of bondage, whether physical, material, spiritual, emotional, or other. It is a total liberation from any type of oppression, exploitation, and violence.[42] As a result, to seek holistic shalom, Christians are called to dismantle the structures of oppression and to transform society so that no one is oppressed and excluded, people who are in need enjoy physical and material well-being, and people can work toward right relationship. Although Yoder does not explicitly state this, in holistic shalom, the right relationship with the environment is also fundamental, because exploiting the environment disrespects the Creator and does injustice to people who rely to natural resources and the surrounding environment. Without the right relationship with nature, there is no shalom.

Becoming an intercultural church community requires the cultivation of shalom, a place where people from diverse socio-cultural, religious, and ethnic backgrounds can learn from one another, help one another, and celebrate with one another because of their differences and not in spite of them. To foster and enhance this mutual shalom, it is necessary to identify types of exclusionary practices and systems operative in the community and to change existing power structures. These endeavours are necessary so that no one cultural and social group dominates; rather, every group must engage actively as they maintain their full dignity and identity, and the interests of all groups are respected and engaged productively as contributors to a common sense of togetherness. Furthermore, shalom is not limited to those people who are already in a community, but also leads all of us to ever-new encounters.

An understanding of shalom that is deeply connected to social order, infrastructure, and systems challenges the systemic evil existing in society and in church communities. It encourages and inspires the creation of non-violent systems of equity and well-being, systems in which there is no oppression and exclusion, and in which marginalized people can feel safe and secure. It also calls the church to embody peace by engaging with people and nature non-violently and participating in social transformation.

By exploring the foundational principle of shalom, this chapter develops a contextual framework for understanding basic themes in interculturality and how differences are grappled with in Canadian multicultural society. It provides a platform for further analysis in chapter 5. I began part 2 by exploring why all theologies are contextual, and I closely surveyed the intrinsic relationship among context, culture, ethnicity, and race. To construct a Mennonite ecclesiology that is empowering, relevant, and appropriate in Canada, I examined one dominant way of dealing with difference through Canadian multiculturalism and its limitations. Although multiculturalism has changed over time, Canadian multiculturalism remains "state multiculturalism," which the government is actively involved in shaping, managing, and promoting. The state uses social, legal, and economic mechanisms to control the definition and practise of multiculturalism. Put differently, multiculturalism is one of the existing dominant ideologies in Canada, and through it the government continues to decide what "counts in society and what does not, what is at the centre and what at the margins, which voices are heard and which silenced."[43] A few different solutions have been proposed, including critical multiculturalism, and Quebec's interculturalism. As another alternative, several church organizations have chosen to respond from a faith perspective and to push the church to become an intercultural institution, believing that it is a better way for the church to engage with difference. Though the term "intercultural" can mean different things in different contexts, Gittins and Caro offer helpful theological definitions. Based on these, I then proposed the notion of shalom, which encompasses *convivencia*, as a foundational intercultural principle from an Anabaptist-Mennonite perspective.

All of these discussions help to situate Mennonite churches in Canada. By virtue of their representing a predominantly white social-religious group, these Mennonite churches are exposed to all of the issues that Canadian multiculturalism addresses. Different circles of Mennonites respond to multiculturalism differently. Some might fully embrace what Canadian multiculturalism aims to do, some might accept only a few aspects of it, and some might reject it totally. Wherever they stand, they must answer some important questions: What does it mean to be a faithful church in Canada? How should we deal with the diversity and difference that exists within and outside of the church? How can we embody an alternative community, a messianic community, and be a witness to peace in this society? From a contextual liberative perspective,

MC Canada must commit to becoming an intercultural church. Based on the history of and ecclesial resources affirmed by Mennonite churches in Canada, how can we do so? What Mennonite theo-ethical resources may be affirmed to empower and transform the church to become intercultural? What beliefs and practices might be a hindrance to a church that desires to become intercultural? What would a Canadian Mennonite intercultural church look like? I address these questions in part 3.

PART THREE

Toward a Critical Intercultural Mennonite Ecclesiology

Building on part 1, and incorporating the critical analysis of culture, race, ethnicity, and faith in the Canadian context elaborated in part 2, in chapter 5 I critically reassess Mennonite peoplehood from a contextual and liberative perspective to provide the material basis for particular guidelines on how Canadian Mennonites can become a critical intercultural community. By analyzing the sources, norms, and frames of three Mennonite theologies – the messianic community, the missional church, and the shalom church – I identify five problematic issues in Mennonite theologies: (1) the sharp contrast between the church and world; (2) the belief that Jesus and the Bible are the final authorities, when in reality, Mennonites reply on other theological sources without recognizing it; (3) a strong emphasis on Christology that dismisses the inclusive nature of God, Jesus, and the Holy Spirit; (4) assuming widely existing norms within the community, such as whiteness, patriarchy, and heteronormativity, which profoundly influence theological discourses; and (5) unconsciously assuming and being complicit in the Northern American colonial project. Furthermore, by reassessing the "experienced" church, I assert that "ethnic myopia" and "lax racial awareness" are impeding the church community from becoming an anti-racist church. In light of this, I claim that instead of dismissing the dominant Mennonite ethnicities, the church should recognize multiple ethnicities and commit to working toward empowering marginalized groups as full participants in the church capable of contributing gifts to Mennonite peoplehood.

As a vehicle for naming, resisting, and transforming these exclusionary practices and problematic issues, in chapter 6 I offer three theo-ethical norms, which are based on the foundational principle of shalom: justice and love, hospitality, and mutuality. These norms can function as guiding frames for the construction of an intercultural Mennonite Church in Canada: working toward intercultural unity, practising radical discipleship and radical hospitality, striving for shalom and prophetic dialogue in multicultural publics, and seeking repentance and reconciliation in Indigenous-settler relations.

5

Critical Reassessment of Mennonite Peoplehood

In Revelation 21:22–27, we encounter a profound and captivating image. The New Jerusalem, the city of the future, is portrayed without a temple, for its temple is the Lord God Almighty and the Lamb. There's no need for the sun or the moon to provide light, as the glory of God itself illuminates the city, and the Lamb serves as its lamp. The nations walk in this divine light, and the kings of the earth bring their glory into it. Its gates remain perpetually open, and the city is bathed in everlasting light. What's particularly intriguing is that nations come bearing their own glory. This aspect of the passage is noteworthy, as in the Bible, "glory" and "honour" are often associated with God. Yet here, we see a reference to "the glory and the honour of the nations."

It's important to note that in the original Greek version of the passage, John uses the word "ethnicity" instead of "nation." For greater accuracy, it should read, "the glory and the honour of the ethnicities." While material wealth is certainly a part of "the glory and the honour," these phrases primarily allude to the cultural richness of each ethnicity. This encompasses their cultural practices, wisdom, and knowledge. Each ethnic group contributes their unique cultural practices and perspectives as they enter the New Jerusalem, thereby glorifying God through their cultural gifts. They enter the city not as culture-less entities, but as fully cultural beings, and their cultural contributions are recognized as elements of glory and honour, enhancing the city's diversity and glorifying God. Negative or harmful cultural practices are left behind, and no abominable or false practices are allowed into the new city.

The vision of Revelation 21 is profoundly powerful. It embraces and celebrates the finest cultural practices of all ethnicities, recognizing them as sources of glory and honour. In this new city, these practices enrich the community and bring glory to God. The New Jerusalem becomes a place of intercultural worship, where people praise God as fully cultural beings.

As various communities, social groups, and cultures possess their unique "glory and honour" alongside various undesirable practices, Mennonite peoplehood also carries its own "glory and honour" as well as negatives practices. Consequently, this chapter is dedicated to the identification of exclusionary practices so that Mennonite churches can abandon them as they continually strive to become a critical intercultural church. Chapter 5 will commence by critically reassessing Mennonite peoplehood from a contextual liberative perspective, offering guidelines based upon the context in which Mennonite churches in Canada find themselves as they contemplate the journey toward interculturality. To reiterate, a contextual liberative approach incorporates critical social theories and analysis to assess various dimensions, including social, cultural, economic, and political factors, dominant ideologies, and power dynamics. It directs our attention toward a path of liberation for marginalized people facing different forms of oppression. In this endeavour, I will begin by analyzing certain tensions in the sources and norms of Mennonite peace theologies (the believed church) before investigating Mennonite peoplehood as a social group encompassing the religious, ethnocultural, and racial dimensions lived out within Canada (the experienced church).

Identifying Problematic Issues in Mennonite Peace Theologies

In chapter 1, three different Mennonite theological frames – the messianic community, the missional church, and the shalom church – were laid out and examined for their ability to offer a robust engagement with difference. Employing a contextual liberative lens, the present chapter highlights five ways that Mennonite perspectives may exclude other voices. For clarification, when I describe these perspectives, I am not making a totalizing claim, suggesting that all Mennonites think and act the same way. Rather, acknowledging the diversity of Mennonite perspectives, I will mostly concentrate on some common views expressed in the relevant literature that are found within Mennonite communities in Northern America.

The first noticeable Mennonite means of exclusivism is based on how Mennonite circles generally frame the relationship between the church and the world. Based on the perspectives of the messianic community and the missional church, the church is depicted as the community that knows the true way of living; thus, it is said to play a key role in teaching the world. There is a sense of superiority in this depiction, rooted in its claims to scriptural purity and a strong Christocentric approach. As explained in chapter 1, according to this understanding, believers need to resist the world, speak prophetic words to it, and not conform to it. The emphasis on how principalities and powers have become corrupted and how the state causes violence amounts to a negative portrayal of the world. As a matter of fact, the Anabaptist movement depicted the world in this manner from its very beginnings. The Schleitheim Confession states that "all those who have fellowship with the dead works of darkness have no part in the light. Thus all who follow the devil and the world, have no part with those who have been called out of the world unto God."[1] This negative depiction of the world can also be seen in *Anabaptist Vision*, a seminal work by Harold Bender, a respected and influential Mennonite leader and scholar active from the 1920s to the 1960s.

John Howard Yoder is aware of how the classic countercultural model within the Mennonite churches can assume its own righteousness "over against" others, a position that may stem from their history of persecution. Hence, in *For the Nations*, he explicitly explains that the church is *for* the world, *for* the nations. In spite of that, he still maintains the view that the world is corrupt and that the church has to point the world toward salvation. In this kind of depiction of the church and the world, active engagement with the latter implies one-way communication rather than a mutual dialogue.

One of the reasons why the messianic community and the missional church perceive the world in this way is because they view the church, at least the faithful church, as a marginal community. They use this posture as vantage point from which to critique the world and society. Mennonites experienced a long history of persecution; as a result, they created their identity based upon a need for self-protection and sought insularity and purity. In light of this, those who colluded with outsiders, persecutors, and/or state leaders were deemed corrupt or compromised. A dualistic logic informs their ecclesiologies, and so it has been important for them to emphasize the uniqueness of the church and the necessity of its separation from the world.[2] However, within the current Northern American context, Christian churches cannot be seen solely as marginal. Though historically marginalized, Mennonites are now integrated into society and enjoy a degree of influence.

Nevertheless, by still maintaining the depiction of their church as a marginalized community that knows the truth, in contrast to a corrupt world, Mennonites may oversimplify their interpretation of the world almost to the point of caricature, and they may lack the ability to recognize other marginal groups in the world, even those who are much more marginalized within the church. Consequently, they can encourage what Emily Ralph Servant calls "gentrification of the margins," in which Mennonites with some privileges identify themselves as marginalized and take up space that should be accorded to other marginalized people. For example, white Mennonites displace people of colour, male Mennonites silence women, and educated Mennonites dominate those in the pews.[3] Also, self-identifying as a victim or a member of an oppressed group can mask Mennonite privilege and lead inadvertently to the further marginalization of other groups. A lack of awareness of privilege makes the task of self-examination seem unimportant or irrelevant. Due to this misperception, those in privileged positions may believe that they stand equally with other marginalized communities while failing to work for change within and outside their communities.

A second way that Mennonites may create exclusionary postures is through their arguments for placing their final authority in Jesus, who is revealed through scripture. Highlighting Jesus can promote inclusion, but by absolutizing one's view of Jesus and scripture as the final and only position available, while overlooking context, reason, and experience as theological sources, can exclude and deny other perspectives, especially those of traditionally marginalized people. When Yoder emphasizes true conversation, he criticizes Roman Catholics for placing their faith in papal authority, and Protestants for relying on dogma drawn from "the Renaissance, the Reformation, the Enlightenment, idealism, the scientific worldview, and a revived Judeo-Christian doctrine of sin ... Greco-Roman ideals of equity ... and Occidental ideals of democracy."[4] After making these criticisms, Yoder writes that in order to have true conversation and unity, Christians need to put their faith in the Jesus who is revealed in scripture, as do the groups in the free church tradition, such as the Swiss and Hutterian Brethren, Baptists, Mennonites, and others. Echoing Yoder's view, *Confession of Faith in a Mennonite Perspective* makes a similar statement: "Other claims on our understanding of Christian faith and life, such as tradition, culture, experience, reason, and political powers, need to be tested and corrected by the light of Holy Scripture."[5]

The choice to put Jesus and the Bible above all other theological sources is a significant mark of the Mennonites. Churches that are part of Protestant traditions also emphasize the primary importance of scripture; nonetheless, Mennonites have a tendency to overlook other theological sources, like tradition, reason, and experience. This because they do not have well-systematized theologies (and some prefer to keep it this way because of the view that following Jesus is more about living out what one believes than articulating one's faith systematically in a written statement), traditions (like those of Greek Orthodox churches), a central leader (like the pope in Catholicism), or authoritative creeds (like a host of other denominations). Mennonites have widely shared confessions, but they do not have the "operative authority in adjudicating theological matters." In Mennonite circles, confessions are used to highlight our common beliefs and those aspects that bind us as a family of faith, but not to officially settle theological debates within the church, nor to dictate what Mennonites must believe.[6]

There is some degree of recognition among Mennonite scholars that all theologies are contextual, that knowledge is situated, and that there is no culture-less interpretation of the gospel. For example, Lois Barrett argues that all theologians understand the Bible through their own lenses, cultures, traditions, experiences, and contexts. This means that there is no pure, plain, neutral, and universal interpretation of the Bible. Yoder admits as much, asserting that scripture cannot be read apart from each reader's specific context. He writes, there "is no such thing as an isolated word of the Bible carrying meaning in itself. It has meaning only when it is read by someone and then only when that reader and the society in which he or she lives can understand the issue to which it speaks."[7] He even argues that while truth is universal, in order for people to perceive and understand it, it should be interpreted and contextualized in a particular setting.[8] He further states that the way Christian conviction is lived out will "differ from one social context to another."[9] Yet, as far as I know, Yoder himself does not explicitly comment on how his own theological perspective and interpretation of the Bible were shaped by his culture, experience, socio-historical context, and other theological sources. Acknowledging one's finite location and eschewing exclusionary claims to a sovereign position over and against others is part of epistemological humility. And more, it is methodologically central to the action-reflection approach inherent in a liberative contextual framework. If this posture of humility is not incorporated, Mennonites are liable to dismiss unfamiliar perspectives by arguing that non-Mennonite theologies are interpreted through their own social and cultural lenses and challenging non-Mennonites to instead have "biblically" based theologies. Mennonites may criticize other groups for utilizing other sources in interpreting Jesus and the Bible while being unaware of how they themselves integrate other sources to interpret the Bible. The resulting inconsistency and contradictions are ironic.

An example helps show the point. In an article for the *Global Anabaptist Mennonite Encyclopedia Online*, Daniel Schipani, a Mennonite scholar and professor, argues that Latin American liberation theologies run the risk of reducing the gospel to a revolutionary ideology, advancing a simplistic interpretation of historical development, encouraging adherents to interpret their social situations mostly through "particular explanations of social struggle and change," and too heavily emphasizing situational pragmatism in the understanding of praxis and truth.[10] Schipani is criticizing liberation theologies for utilizing sources like Marxism and other critical social theories in interpreting Jesus and the Bible, but he seems unaware of the extent to which Mennonites of European descent draw on their own white, Western, and middle-class experience to interpret the Bible.[11] Acknowledging contextuality does not mean that Mennonites have to give up to their aspiration to treat scripture as the final authority. But it may mean they need to recognize that they are utilizing (explicitly or implicitly) other theological sources, and that perspectives shaped by their own social locations and ethnocultural backgrounds are deeply ingrained in their interpretation of the Bible.

A third way that Mennonites may exclude other voices is through a theological view in which the Bible, mission, discipleship, ecclesiology, and other theologies are interpreted mainly through a narrow Christological lens. Christocentrism does not lead to exclusion per se, but in a kind of Jesuology, which predominantly focuses on identifying the "authentic" followers of Jesus and how the disciples should act and believe within the church, it dismisses and/or de-emphasizes the inclusive nature of God, Jesus, and the Holy Spirit. Fernando Enns explains that while the historic peace churches, including Mennonites, have contributed much to ecumenical dialogue and have invited other denominations to expand their understanding of peace, at the same time, they have limitations, particularly the Mennonites' Christocentric perspective. Enns asserts, "we have at times restricted our *theo*logy to *Christ*ology, or even to '*Jesu*ology.' Our predominant and exclusive image of the church has therefore been the church as the discipling body of Christ."[12] As a result, Mennonites dismiss the continuation of the election of the people of Israel, and how the Holy Spirit works in other religions and in all creation. Hence, Enns argues for a more Trinitarian approach to Mennonite theology, especially in ecclesiology, to underscore the inclusive nature of God. Noticing that the Trinity is largely absent in the Mennonite tradition, some Mennonite theologians are moving beyond strict Christocentrism. For example, in *Images of the Church in Mission*, John Driver employs a Trinitarian approach, foregrounding the active role of the Holy Spirit and offering several images, such as "the people of God," "Sojourners," and "the family of God," that directly relate to God. Another example is Norman Kraus. He emphasizes a much larger role for the Holy Spirit in his book *The Community of the Spirit*. Nonetheless, it is still true that, overall, Mennonite theologies have a strong Christocentric view.[13] Consequently, in narrow terms, this may lead to limited engagement with other religious traditions, non-faith communities, and ecological concerns, Enns asserts, because these themes are outside of the realm of the church. This particular Christology does not provide enough common ground for constructive dialogue. Accordingly, it cultivates an insular ecclesiology, which then feeds resistance to intercultural engagement because of an oppositional attitude to "the world" and to the things outside of the body of Christ.

A fourth way that voices may be excluded is by assuming, tacitly as well as overtly, the widely existing norms within the Mennonite community: whiteness, patriarchy, and heteronormativity. Although Mennonites in Northern America are becoming more diverse, as mentioned in chapter 1, white men are still dominant within the Mennonite Church, and feminist scholars like Lydia Harder, Carol Penner, Kim Penner, and others continually argue that the church is still patriarchal. Also, even though some effort has been made to be more inclusive, the church still maintains heteronormativity. Mennonites can confess that Jesus is the new norm that they follow, and this is a valuable aspiration. Yet they must still identify unspoken countervailing norms that cause harm, using power analysis and the lens of intersectionality; these norms diminish the witness of the gospel. It is crucial to name and work to change such countervailing norms and seek alternatives, or else Mennonite witness and practices are limited by the marginalization and exclusion of different voices. For example, Mennonites can preach about the priesthood of all believers and about the communal biblical hermeneutic, but the whiteness, patriarchy, and heteronormativity existing in our church will determine who may be at the table and who may not. In theory, the hermeneutic of community emphasizes the mutual communication and interactive search for truth, so that a variety of convictions and multiple individual interpretations of God and the Bible contribute to the community's identity and theology. Despite this ideal aspiration, as Lydia Harder argues, the hermeneutic community was controlled by white men for years; so, even though it claims to be a praxis inviting all voices and views, it was instead used to resist transformation and to maintain the status quo.[14] Mennonites might celebrate that they seriously listen to everyone at the table while being unaware of who has been filtered out or who did not come because they felt unsafe at the table. Hence, naming and resisting countervailing norms is crucial for living into the believed church's aspiration of welcome for all.

Finally, a fifth way that Mennonites may exclude voices is by unconsciously accepting and perpetuating the Western colonial project. Such unawareness can lead to exclusion and can perpetuate settler colonialism. Currently, through the Indigenous-Settler Relations program established by MC Canada, local churches are becoming aware of settler colonialism in Canada and learning to commit to the Truth and Reconciliation Commission's Calls to Action. Yet, because the mechanism of colonialism was not recognized for most of the Mennonites' long historic presence in Canada, Mennonite theologians tend not to engage the topic or the relationship between Mennonite settlers and Indigenous people. This issue links with the first and the third forms of exclusivism outlined above. Since the church is called to resist the world and focus primarily on edifying the body of Christ, Mennonites have a tendency to see themselves as separate from the world. Hence, they do not critically examine the ways in which they are actually complicit with the violence of the state. Even the discourse of the missional church, in which understanding context is pivotal, does not mention Christians of European ancestry living in the legacy of colonialism and colonialism's continued influence on contemporary society.

In the early years, when Mennonites migrated to North America as persecuted refugees, they were given land that had been dispossessed from Indigenous people. While Mennonites have not directly participated in the colonial project of taking the land away from Indigenous people; rather, they have participated in the project by living on and benefiting from the land and by omitting Indigenous justice. These issues are discussed far too infrequently, at least in the messianic community, the missional church, and the shalom church. As a result, Mennonites end up excluding the voices of Indigenous people and being complicit in the violence of settler colonialism.

Re-examining Mennonite Peoplehood through Critical Social Theories

As in the previous section, by incorporating critical analysis of culture, ethnicity, and race performed in chapter 3, the present section aims to problematize the sense of Mennonite peoplehood and identity as a narrowly defined ethnic and racial group in order to guide the church in becoming intercultural. In a close examination of experienced Mennonite peoplehood, two main issues emerge as barriers hindering Mennonite churches' engagement with difference: Mennonite ethnicity and whiteness. These are not problems in and of themselves; what makes them problematic in the Canadian Mennonite context is what I call "ethnic myopia" and "lax racial awareness."

As I stated in the introduction, Royden Loewen describes six ways in which different Mennonite groups have dealt with and positioned themselves in relation to the issues of ethnicity and faith: (1) embracing ethnicity while de-emphasizing religious tradition; (2) accepting Mennonite ethnicity while disdaining traditional Mennonite religiousness; (3) separating ethnicity from religious faith, and fully supporting Mennonite faith while trying to push Mennonite ethnicity aside; (4) linking Mennonite faith and Mennonite ethnicity; (5) recognizing that Mennonite ethnicity is symbolic and without religious significance, while seeming to exist almost naturally alongside Mennonite religious faith; and (6) identifying as Mennonites but not as a Mennonite ethnicity or as a Anabaptist faith. Based on the discourse of faith and ethnicity in Mennonite circles, it seems like the issues of faith and ethnicity will persist, and that the majority of Mennonites in Northern America will continue to view their Mennonite ethnic identity as crucial. From this perspective, the predominant Mennonite groups deal seriously with the interconnection between faith and ethnicity. However, these groups tend not to incorporate the ethnicities of other non-traditional Mennonite church members. I refer to this phenomenon as ethnic myopia because within the inner circle – Mennonites of Swiss, German, Dutch, and/or Russian background – ethnicities are clearly recognized and valued, and they are carefully documented by various scholars and theologians who write for the public about how these ethnicities have shaped Mennonite faith. Nonetheless, ethnicities of outer circles (i.e., Mennonites from non-traditional ethnicities) are not integrated into, or even considered part of, the larger Mennonite identity.

The fact that white European histories are considered foundational for Mennonites is part of the problem. I say "part" because it is true that the history of Mennonites in Europe is formative. However, this history proves to have a constricting hold over how "other stories and histories" become mapped onto the landscape of identity. A privileging of "foundational" ethnicities determines which ethnicities count as Mennonite – that is, those cultural and historical traditions whose ancestry links directly with what are seen as "originary" Mennonite traditions with European roots. This appeal to "foundational ethnicity" is constructed, to be sure, and is a way to mark and create an insular heritage against distillation and compromise. It becomes a protective strategy bolstered by countercultural ecclesiologies. This is how the ethnic consciousness discussed in chapter 3 is being played out in the Mennonite circles. As a result, the dominant Mennonite groups have what I call ethnic myopia. As mentioned in the introduction, this causes people who are not ethnically Mennonite to feel that they are second-class church members and therefore not "Mennonite" enough.

From a contextual liberative perspective, as seen in chapter 3, faith, culture, ethnicity, and race are intrinsically connected. The link between ethnicity and faith is not a problem since no theologian can speak beyond his or her ethnocultural perspective. The problem is that in the Mennonite discourse of faith and ethnicity, the latter tends mostly, if not always, to focus on the people from Swiss, German, Dutch, and/or Russian backgrounds, without considering other ethnic groups that exist within our diverse church community. If minoritized ethnic groups are invoked, they are generally tokenized and/or seen as people who need the "help" of the dominant group. In my own local church, there are Chinese, Korean, Peruvian, Argentinian, Cuban, Colombian, and Paraguayan Mennonites, but their ethnicities have not been integrated into the discourse of Mennonite ethnicity. If Mennonites are simply an ethnic group and not a religious community, then there is no need to have this discussion, because a community characterized by ethnicity alone does not have the moral obligation to become an inter-ethnic community. However, because Mennonites are already open to other ethnocultural diversities, and since the Bible calls the church to be a body of many members, its ecclesial structures has to reflect that diversity. This requires the construction of an intercultural church, one that moves beyond tokenism and patronization.

Based on my observation and experience, as a person who has been a Mennonite for fifteen years and has served in various leadership roles, Mennonite churches in Northern America do indeed welcome people from different ethnic groups. As a result, some of these people become active church members and leaders. However, they are still not fully integrated into the discourse of Mennonite identity and ethnicity. If Mennonite churches genuinely seek to engage with difference, they must welcome people from different ethnic groups and develop mechanisms to reimagine together what it means to be Mennonite, both religiously and ethnically. Engaging difference means co-constructing Mennonite identity and theologies as well.

Although numerous writings discuss Mennonite ethnicity, *whiteness* within Mennonite communities has not been explored enough. After arriving in Canada, white Mennonites were marginalized for their religious and political views. They were also subsequently discriminated against because of their ethnicity, especially those of German background during the First and Second World Wars. They have not, however, ever been persecuted or mistreated because of their whiteness. Tobin Miller Shearer, a historian who examines racism in Mennonite churches, notes that Mennonites of European descent prefer to view themselves not as a racial community but as a religious one.[15] Jill Stoltzfus also explains that Mennonites "tend to most strongly define themselves in terms of their common historical and spiritual experiences and the multiple contexts in which these experiences have occurred."[16] Consequently, Mennonites tend not to focus on the implications of their roles as members of the largest racial group in Canada, where whites are still the dominant group with much more control of political, economic, and social power. Noticing this, Malinda Berry asserts that white Mennonites

> Do not think of themselves as sitting on top of the food chain. They think of themselves as the quiet in the land, as displaced refugees, conscientious objectors ridiculed by non-pacifist neighbors, war-tax resisters. However true these identities have been, they should not mask the fact that European Mennonites are white, and being white has political relevance, just as being African American, Asian, Hispanic, and Native American does.[17]

As Sara Ahmed writes, "whiteness is only invisible for those who inhabit it, or those who get so used to its inhabitance that they learn not to see it, even when they are not it."[18] Whiteness is more than a racial classification. It is "a social and institutional status and identity imbued with legal, political, economic, and social rights and privileges that are denied to others."[19] In Canada and the United States, whiteness has been constructed through particular historical, socio-political, economic, and ethnocultural processes, including European colonization and slavery. Being white in Canada, one enjoys white privilege, and this is tied into white dominance that is prevalent in society, although not all whites experience the same level of privilege, as in the way that francophone Canadians feel discriminated against by their anglophone counterparts. Jennifer Harvey, a Christian ethicist, describes whiteness as a

> phenomenon that can exist only with the direct involvement and complicit participation of white people. At the same time, it is also

> larger and more powerful than the individual white person, having taken on a life of its own. In other words, regardless of one's beliefs, commitments, and even one's actions, white people cannot simply "opt out" of whiteness. To speak of whiteness is to name the reality that the light-skinned among us (people categorized as "white") are implicated in perpetrating and perpetuating white supremacy, however actively or passively. To speak of whiteness is to explicitly name the reality that white people live out real choices in relation to agency-filled racism and racial issues and to state that white people have a particular and active relationship to white supremacy and racial injustice.[20]

Harvey comments that, ironically, when white people avoid, ignore, and deny naming and contending with whiteness, it is most powerfully at work. Further, the fact that white people can do this is evidence of structural support for whiteness – that is, white supremacy – because people of colour are mindful of and unable to ignore whiteness. White supremacy is the structural and ideological mechanisms that protect and perpetuate white dominance, keeping the status quo firmly in place. In a society dominated by white supremacy, "whiteness covers up the very connections we must see and disrupt if we are to make genuine progress toward racial justice."[21] As a result, whiteness should be named and contended with among Mennonite churches in Canada, whose members should discuss the ways in which they are complicit with white supremacy in society and how whiteness has shaped the local churches. Complicity is the state of being involved in unjust or wrong activity. While one can actively and intentionally be complicit, it can also be done passively and unintentionally. An example of this is the white Mennonites who taught in and helped operate Indian residential schools in Canada: in so doing, they were complicit in the cultural genocide of Indigenous people, in spite of their belief in peace.

Mennonites of colour in Northern America have been problematizing whiteness and the racism existing within their communities since the 1950s. The earliest document that problematized whiteness in this was by Vincent Harding, a pastor of African descent and a civil rights activist, who in 1959 called the churches to stop "slavishly and silently" conforming to the racism and segregation practised by whites.[22] Another person of colour, John Ventura, a Latino pastor, accused church leaders of failing to support Latino congregations and their development.[23] Harding, Ventura, and other marginalized pastors and leaders challenged members of the white Mennonite community to examine themselves through a racial lens. In response to several social and political factors, including efforts to pass the Civil Rights Act, beginning in the 1960s a host of statements were brought forth from various Mennonite communities.[24] Analyzing how white Mennonites responded to racism and white identity in their churches and in organizations like the Mennonite Central Committee between 1960 and 1985, Shearer notes that white Mennonites were inclined to identify themselves as white only in the face of conflict and when they felt compelled to do so. For instance, in the aftermath of Martin Luther King Jr's assassination, several Mennonite leaders published statements arguing that white people must fight against white racism and white supremacy. Yet, soon after, everything went back to the old ways; church leadership, staff, and board members in Mennonite churches and organizations remained exclusively white.[25] Once conflicts related to race abated, white Mennonites stopped identifying themselves as white and returned to their regular lifestyles. As a result, their anti-racism work was mostly reactive rather than proactive. To identify this phenomenon, I employ the term "lax racial awareness." Lax racial awareness is problematic because the work toward racial justice is an ongoing endeavour, and by its very nature cannot be purely reactive. Without developing a prolonged acknowledgment of their white identity, the ways in which they benefit from white privilege, and their complicity in white dominance, white Mennonites will not be able to engage genuinely in anti-racist work because that work consists in transforming the social system and institutions that are based on white power and privilege. It is symptomatic of white privilege for white Mennonites to be able to relax their racial awareness, whereas racialized Mennonites are constantly reminded that they cannot be part of the inner group because of their skin colour. White supremacy makes lax racial awareness possible because of the structures that normalize whiteness, and in this context lax racial awareness becomes "strategic forgetfulness," which is deliberate and racist in character.

Jeffrey Gingerich's dissertation, which is based on a historical and ethnographic study, shows that the attempt to "transcend" racial identity and to be "racially colour-blind" will not resolve the issue of racism within the

Mennonite Church.[26] Based on his qualitative research on twenty-one congregations in the multicultural city of Philadelphia, Pennsylvania, where eleven different languages are spoken as primary languages, Gingerich observes that to evade discussion on white identity and racism, white Mennonite leaders have shifted the focus of their "identity to the universal qualities of religious identity and the celebration of ethnic difference. This was accompanied by a move toward an evangelical identity."[27] One would assume that this move toward broader parameters of identity would create much more inclusive and welcoming communities and more engaging relationships among different ethnic and racial groups; but, paradoxically, this ended up leading to a more "particularistic style of worship and organization within the separate ethnic congregations."[28] The local churches stressed a broader and "common identity" but utilized religious symbols adapted to the emotional and spiritual needs of the majority. The emphasis on this broader identity ended up leading local churches to be ethnically and racially segregated. Appeals to "unity" are often based on a notion of inclusion predicated on very limited terms. As a result, many non-whites who were seeking a place to belong found it difficult to be in churches where whites were the majority – and so they ended up not attending Mennonite churches or seeking out Mennonite churches in which their own ethnicity or races constituted the majority. Although Gingerich's research is limited to Mennonite congregations in Philadelphia, his findings are helpful because they show that racial difference and issues of race cannot be adequately dealt with by being racially colour-blind or by seeking a broader identity like Mennonite faith. To create a genuinely inclusive and intercultural community, as Gingerich's research demonstrates, it is crucial – especially for white Christians – to acknowledge our racial and ethnocultural identities, and together, to strive to become anti-racist.

Segregated worship gathering is troubling because it is a form of racism. However, racism can also be explicitly and implicitly at work even in an ostensibly "intercultural" church and form of worship. Traci West points out how racial divisions and inequities can take place within a worship service in a predominantly white church – for example, in church prayer or an announcement about mission:

> Ideas might be conveyed about who the normal, regular (white) people are, and who should be assumed to be the (racial) others.

> Racialized understandings of "us and them" can be strongly conveyed in prayers about those who are "less fortunate than we are" or projects to reach out to help "them." These practices exemplify ritualized responses to local community and global needs, and teach the congregation to recognize its distinctive Christian identity on a weekly basis. They also link Christian identity to a sense of privilege that easily merges with racial messages about privilege in the broader culture.[29]

Even from these aspects of worship service, racial divisions can occur implicitly and explicitly. Although inclusive terms like "we" and/or "the church" are used, they will not work to overcome the "us and them" dynamic that exist in the church. Until church leaders intentionally commit to changing the norm of whiteness that exists in the church and intentionally seek to form an anti-racist and intercultural community, nonwhite members will merely be seen as people to be assimilated into the dominant church culture or as objects of charity.

Another example of how racism can manifest in a church is when a white person thanks God and gives testimony to the congregation about the "blessings" that they have received from God while not being aware that these blessings could have been received from our racist society with its exploitation of marginalized communities.[30] Without critical examination, saying "amen" and celebrating with the person who is giving thanks can be a means for the church to deny and even support cultural and systemic racism in our society. For this reason, it is crucial to name whiteness and white privilege and to critically reimagine church worship rituals and practices, including missional and theological dimensions.

Mennonites in white society are called to go beyond lax racial awareness to anti-racism, engaging in allyship with racialized communities to dismantle white supremacy and racism within and outside the church. However, Tobin Miller explains that there are at least six approaches that limit white Mennonites' effective participation in anti-racist work. Thus, it is important to name these approaches, recognize how they function to limit white Mennonites' anti-racist work, and find ways to resist and overcome them. The first approach is the tradition of martyrdom, which causes some Mennonites to think that they are different from other white racist Christians because they have been living mostly as a persecuted or marginalized people. Some think that they are powerless and therefore cannot bring social transformation; hence, they miss opportunities to engage in anti-racist work. Second, there is a tendency among white Mennonites to avoid overt conflict. Interestingly, this intersects with white fragility's aversion to conflict and/or being shamed. This creates shallow unity and false harmony, and it encourages passive-aggressive behaviour. Since it is crucial to have honest conversations about racism, both within and outside the church, this style of engaging in (or avoiding) conflict becomes an obstacle. Third, as discussed earlier in this chapter, the strong contrast between the state and the church causes many Mennonites to believe that they are different from mainstream racist society. A countercultural mentality perceives itself as free from all the societal ills and so assumes it is not complicit with the world. Also, since the believed church is "without spot or wrinkle," most problems are thought to be found in society rather than the church.[31] This influences Mennonites to believe that they are not a part of or complicit in colonialism, nationalism, white supremacy, and racism. Fourth, the strong familial network in Mennonite communities encourages white people to remain among other white ethnic Mennonites, without needing to work and interact with people from other backgrounds. This dynamic is part of the very fabric of white privilege. Thus, white Mennonites do not perceive the injustices experienced by people of colour and they do not create authentic relationships with non-white people. The fifth approach is the Mennonite belief in "service superiority." Through several Mennonite organizations, young and old people travel overseas to offer their services; they believe that they have done a better job than other white Christians by emphasizing the creation of strong relationships with local communities. When they return, they assume that they know the people and the culture of these communities well enough. Consequently, they miss the opportunity to critically reflect on precisely how they are embedded in the mechanisms of white supremacy and colonialism. Sixth, a moderate level of shunning occurs when people demand too much change from their community.[32] Those who perpetrate this form of shunning refuse to listen to diverse perspectives and thus foreclose further conversation. This blocks anti-racist efforts to bring about change. Naming, recognizing, and overcoming these approaches are imperative if the church is to become an anti-racist community.

The key point here is that *intercultural* engagement and practice in a white-dominant society and church is at the same time an inherently *anti-racist* engagement and practice. This means that becoming an intercultural church is akin to becoming an anti-racist church. And it involves white Mennonites' ongoing acknowledgment of how they have benefited from white privilege. Moving beyond this racial recognition means white Mennonites take seriously their role in cultivating self-awareness, critiquing mechanisms that restrict active involvement in anti-racist work, refusing to remain silent, and resisting and overcoming systemic racism in church and society.

In this section, I have critiqued ethnic myopia and lax racial awareness. To overcome ethnic myopia, some churches have attempted to embrace a broader identity, like the evangelical identity, emphasizing theological, spiritual, and biblical identity factors rather than socio-political and ethnocultural factors. However, these efforts are problematic because they tend to ignore the fact that the traditional Mennonite ethnic groups are dominant and do not fully consider the rich ethnic perspectives of non-dominant groups. As an alternative, I argue for an intercultural church in which power sharing, concern for equity, mutual welcome, and the participation of all ethnicities are sustained. In this community, people from diverse ethnocultural groups together co-create Mennonite identity. To resolve the issue of lax racial awareness, some churches have attempted to avoid racism and whiteness in Mennonite churches by focusing on their theological, spiritual, and biblical identities. However, as with ethnicity, emphasizing their spiritual/theological identities has only caused white Mennonites to deny racist practices and create segregated communities. Therefore, it is vital for white Mennonites to continually acknowledge their white identity and strive to be an anti-racist church, while recognizing that common practices and shortcomings within the church can limit them in this endeavour. Again, to be an intercultural church means to be an anti-racist church in white dominant society.

I have identified and critically reassessed particular issues of Mennonite peoplehood, both in the believed and the experienced church. These challenges call Mennonite churches to live out their faith in a more liberative and contextual manner, which involves becoming a critical intercultural church that is both decolonizing and anti-racist in Canada, one that fully engages differences, shares power fairly, and challenges binary and exclusionary thoughts and practices. The foundational principle of interculturality, shalom, helps us to reimagine what a genuine church is, thus helping us to become an intercultural church. Incorporating these insights, I will now offer three theo-ethical norms that resonate and correlate with Mennonite ecclesiologies, but which also correct certain pervasive distortions so that Mennonite churches can embrace and apply these norms more fully in their specific contexts. These norms will provide more relevant, appropriate, empowering, and faithful ways for Mennonites to live out their ecclesial calling and theological imagination in Canadian multicultural society.

Theo-ethical Norms in Mennonite Perspective

Naming dominant norms that exist within our community is crucial. There is a difference between naming as a purely descriptive exercise and naming as prescriptive endeavour. The former uncovers existing norms – some of which are harmful or unproductive and serve to maintain the status quo in the form of such phenomena as ableism, heterosexism, or white supremacy. The latter, by contrast, seeks to disrupt and propose alternative and regulative norms. In critically reassessing the contours of Mennonite peoplehood, I first descriptively named dominant operative norms and then problematized them. Now, I seek to prescriptively outline and propose alternative theo-ethical norms rooted in Mennonite theology and intercultural understanding.

Norms are "the criteria of judgment about the sort of persons we ought to be and the sort of actions we ought to perform."[33] Since norms function as ideals, some cases can expose double standards and reveal tensions between beliefs that are actually held and what are aspirational. For example, in *Mennonite Women in Canada*, Marlene Epp explains how Mennonite churches had a double standard of nonconformity. During the first half of the twentieth century, men were allowed to wear clothes that "conformed" to modern society, and they had much more freedom in terms of how they were expected to act in public; yet the churches demanded that women "nonconform" in terms of what they wore and how they acted in public.[34] This double standard with respect to nonconformity occurred because males were the dominant group and had the power to define what conformity was and was not, and were thus able to determine who needed to conform and who to be "nonconformed." Another example is the praxis of the hermeneutic community, which was mentioned earlier in this chapter. Even though it is a praxis aimed at inviting and incorporating all voices and views, as Harder claims, it was controlled by white men and used for several years to resist transformation and to maintain the status quo.[35] These examples show how certain kinds of norms are connected to power and can form and malform the church. Norms can also place limits on our aspired practices and exclude other people. Hence, feminist Mennonites are challenging male-dominant norms, and racialized Mennonites are challenging white Mennonites to "nonconform" and to resist racism.

Given these complexities, what particular kinds of theo-ethical norms can MC Canada articulate as it works to become an intercultural church? In light of the foundational principle of interculturality, shalom, I propose that the church embrace the theo-ethical norms of hospitality, justice and love, and mutuality. These norms are embedded in the understanding of shalom, and their ultimate objective, or *telos*, is to create shalom. They form a kind of constellation through intersecting themes. Although each of them is also contested and limited, these concepts provide valuable parameters that can guide thinking about the relationship between ethnocultural and racial differences without absolutizing or ignoring these differences. They inform us how to mutually live together, relate to each other, and build a community where everyone involved can fully be themselves and also fully open to others. These theo-ethical norms are fundamental to Mennonite traditions, even if they are not explicitly thematized, and they show how insights about interculturality can contribute in ways that fruitfully supplement traditional Mennonite theological perspectives. The following discussion explores each of these norms in Mennonite terms to demonstrate their deep connection with Mennonite traditions, and more, to show how Mennonite praxes and theologies can constructively open into practices of interculturality.

Hospitality is a rich concept in the Bible and has been part of the Christian tradition from the beginning, although it is not a uniquely Christian practice. The Hebrew Bible depicts Israelites as the people who experienced God's salvation and hospitality, and thus are commanded by God to also welcome strangers; examples include passages like Deuteronomy 10:18–19, Leviticus 24:22, Leviticus 12:9–10, and Exodus 23:9. Since there are those who offer hospitality (the hosts) and those who receive it (the guests or strangers), power asymmetry is inevitable in the guest-host relationship. Still, this relationship can move toward mutuality as an ideal, as exemplified by Jesus. Cathy Ross notes, in the four Gospels, Jesus is viewed as a "gracious host, welcoming children, tax collectors, prostitutes and sinners into his presence and therefore offending those who would prefer such guests not to be at his gatherings. But Jesus is also portrayed as vulnerable guest and needy stranger."[36] Observing that Jesus placed himself as both guest and host during his ministry, Christine Pohl comments that this "intermingling of guest and host roles in the person of Jesus is part of what makes the story of hospitality so compelling for Christians."[37]

Hospitality can certainly be distorted, and thus create a dichotomy between host and guest that enables claims to ownership and belonging. This is problematic because, as Canadian theologian Thomas Reynolds notes, the practice can end up becoming a paternalistic act – heightening the position of the host, the giver, and rendering the guest a passive receiver, a gesture to whom freedom and agency are denied.[38] Avoiding this approach involves more than a simple dialogue and sharing of space. Hospitality should be practised mutually. Reynolds explains that hospitality is "Not only about the host welcoming, but welcoming the guest's way of welcoming, as a companion with equal dignity in humanity and whose presence may bring unanticipated transformation. Created is a liminal zone of mutuality, a kind of covenantal exchange happens: both receive and give."[39] This mutual hospitality means that guests also have gifts to share with their hosts, and through this exchange of gifts, each of us is enriched and transformed in a way that moves beyond simple binaries and toward a genuine sharing of power.

When practising hospitality, it is vital to recognize that all people are in different power relationships and are situated differently in their social locations. For this reason, Letty Russell asserts that

> There are many factors that lead people to disagree. It is not just doctrine, or just Scripture, or just the community of faith. It is our differing class, race, gender, ability, age, and sexual identity and orientation ... To welcome another person or group is to look beneath the surface of what they say and do, to understand "where

> they are coming from," and to address the social context out of which the conversation comes.[40]

For Russell, it is through the authentic practise of hospitality that the prevailing power dynamic between host and guest is levelled out, becoming a mutual welcoming practice in which everyone can fully participate. This type of hospitality demands Christian communities provide food, clothing, and shelter to the homeless, and to welcome strangers to our sanctuaries. But it also demands resistance to oppression, working for full human life and dignity, breaking down barriers, and living in unity with those who have been at the margins of church and society.[41]

Hospitality does not simply create space to include marginalized people in the structure and culture of the "host" or dominant social group. Rather, it moves toward co-creating a new structure and culture together. Moreover, Christians engage in this practice not only because they are called to engage in it, or because it is a required part of living together in diverse communities and society, but also because the "guest," the "stranger," or the "other" challenges and calls people out of their complacencies and Christian ghettos, offering them new ways of creating just communities where discomfort is part of prophetic growth.[42]

As noted in chapter 2's exploration of Mennonite history in Canada, it is clear that Mennonites have long held to the norm of hospitality, which can be seen in their active assistance to refugees and provision of mutual aid through MCC and other Mennonite organizations. This norm is based on their belief that they are called to welcome others because they have first been welcomed by the ultimate host, God; also, many of their ancestors were welcomed as they left their birth countries and settled in Canada. In Mennonite theologies and notions of the messianic community, the missional church, and the shalom church, the theme of hospitality is both explicit and implicit. For example, when Yoder writes about the five practices of the church, he explains how important it is to cherish diversity, treat each person equally, understand that everyone is valuable and has gifts to offer, provide an equal opportunity to speak, and especially to take care of the least-honoured people in the community. One problem with Yoder's understanding of hospitality, however, is that it does not concretely identify who these least-honoured people are, nor does it explain what causes them to be designated as such. Furthermore, he does not explore the material power structure of the church. He discusses how power needs to be decentralized and how church ministries should not be performed by only a few gifted people; he writes that the church is to be a place where "there would be no one ungifted, no one not called, no one not empowered, and no one dominated."[43] But he does not examine specific structures of power or offer alternative analyses of what empowerment might mean and how church systems and policies can prevent the church from developing in "the fullness of Christ."

The theo-ethical norm of justice and love is also vital for building right relationships that confront oppression. Justice and love are seen throughout the Bible, and they are foundational to the Christian faith.

Three classical aspects of love are eros, philia, and agape; agape especially has been emphasized in Christian teaching. In a context where agape has historically been highlighted as the paramount expression of Christian love, some have misinterpreted love as unhealthy self-denial, powerlessness, or passive subordination. To avoid this unhealthy understanding, many Christian ethicists have rejected an understanding of love that is limited to self-sacrifice, and instead advocate for love as premised on mutuality and equality. Some scholars avoid offering a clear definition of love because it might be understood merely in abstract terms, obscuring the proper focus on "the object of love – of who and what we love."[44] Thus, these scholars offer descriptions, rather than strict definitions, of love. Some describe love not merely as a sentiment but also as a series of concrete actions operating on the level of both intellect/mind/reason and emotion/heart/passion. It seeks for a mutual relationship – power with instead of power over – and strives for the well-being of all who partake in relationship. Since a healthy loving relationship requires us to examine mutuality and power sharing, this naturally gives rise to the theme of justice.

Theories of justice in Western societies can generally be broken down into three categories: rationalist (Plato, Aristotle, Descartes) and natural law (Thomas Aquinas, Cicero, Ulpian) theories; analytical (Bertrand Russell, G.E. Moore, Ludwig Wittgenstein) and positive (Thomas Hobbes, Chaim Perelman) theories; and utilitarian (Jeremy Bentham, John Stuart Mill, and John Rawls) and other related theories.[45] These theories are invaluable, and some aspects of them can be found in the Bible. However, Christian feminists like Carter Heyward and Elizabeth

Johnson appreciate how the ideas of justice found in the Hebrew and Christian Bibles emphasize relational aspects and focus on care for the well-being of all living beings. This biblical justice requires, for example, that believers give preferential treatment to poor and marginalized people; transform relational and social injustice; stand against any kind of oppression, domination, or exclusion; and actively create and sustain life-giving relationships.[46] Each of these concerns emphasize human relationships, the well-being of all creations, and social justice.

As love is well integrated into the biblical notion of justice, Margaret Farley explains that justice and love supplement one another. She argues for "just love," wherein justice is present when we care for others, and love is present when we seek justice. Justice becomes mechanistic and inhumane without love, making it impossible to secure the full well-being of people and community. At the same time, love becomes sentimental or asymmetrical without justice, which can expose people to abusive relationships.[47] Marvin Ellison offers a complementary analysis through the concept of "justice-love." Ellison explains that justice-love seeks right relations with others and works to "set right all wrong relations, especially distorted power dynamics of domination and subordination."[48] In line with Ellison, Marilyn Legge, a Canadian theologian, explains further that justice-love takes into consideration the human longing for psycho-spiritual and bodily well-being to imagine right relations with others, which requires "mutual respect and care and a fair sharing of power."[49] Elements of love such as affection, openness, giving, and embodiment are balanced with elements of justice like fairness, equity, respect, and rightness. This notion gives equal importance to both body and mind, the personal and the public, and intimate and social relations.

Regardless of whether one favours the term "justice-love" or "just love," both elements are required features of intercultural relationships and community. Seeking justice and love in diverse communities where power is not shared equally calls us to be in solidarity with those who are more marginalized – because justice and love call us to favour the poor and oppressed. Being in solidarity with difference moves us toward a just world "where there is a place for all peoples and where human dignity and human rights become possible."[50] In working toward a common good, it is crucial to avoid reducing difference among people or homogenizing different cultural groups.

In the Mennonite understanding of shalom, the theo-ethical norm of justice and love is already embedded. The core practice of non-violence is actually rooted in love – toward life and toward our enemies. Also, according to Driedger and Kraybill, the norm of love is found in the works of four major Mennonite scholars, Guy F. Hershberger, John Howard Yoder, Lawrence Burkholder, and Gordon Kaufman.[51] Complementing love, the prophetic role of the church, including in speaking against principalities and powers, is based on justice. Historically, Mennonites did not emphasize social justice, but from the early 1970s, they began to show increasing interest in justice, and they have subsequently integrated it deeply into their theology.[52] Justice and love are interconnected threads woven into the work that Mennonites do, such as supporting refugees, working for safety and security, advocating changes in government policy, and building peace. Even so, justice and love invites Mennonites to avoid making a sharp distinction between the church and the world, as doing so results in an "us" versus "them" dynamic, which limits genuine engagement between the church and the world, as discussed in chapter 3. Furthermore, justice and love encourage Mennonites to identify marginalized groups that exist within our church and society, to be in solidarity with them, to interrogate and unmask those forces that pushes these groups to the margin, and to work for justice in seeking their concrete spiritual and bodily well-being.

Although mutuality is assumed in justice and love and is necessary for hospitality, we must also consider it explicitly; if we do not, we neglect many significant ethical aspects, such as power dynamics and concerns for the thriving of all involved in any situation.[53] For this reason, mutuality is another crucial theo-ethical norm. Dawn Nothwehr defines mutuality as "the sharing of 'power-with' by and among all parties in a relationship in a way that recognizes the wholeness and particular experience of each participant toward the end of optimum flourishing of all."[54] The ideal of mutuality can be applied to and further deepened in our understanding of truth, the moral subject, and the good. Mutuality in dialogue raises our consciousness of the limitations of social location and ethnocultural background, helping to identify biases and opening possibilities for learning across difference. Also, humans are interdependent and inter-subjective moral beings rather than merely autonomous and isolated. Hence, we make moral decisions in relationship to others.

Moreover, by recognizing the importance of mutuality in human relationships, our understanding of what is good shifts from an atomistic individualism to a vision that strives to include everyone and all creation. The concept of mutuality invites people to seek truth reciprocally and to be responsible moral agents who make ethical decisions in dialogue with and in acknowledgment of our interdependency. In the process of discerning a common good and the means of pursuing that goal, joint and collaborative norms become salient. Such norms reflect shalom and *convivencia*.

Mutuality is implied in shalom, hospitality, justice, and love, but it is important to explicate it as a distinct norm because it focuses on the means of such practices, and *how* to practise them. Without the qualifier of mutuality, all these practices can lead to harmful, unjust, and oppressive relationships. Human history is filled with enough examples of how the desire to help others under the name of Jesus, mission, justice, love, or peace in fact brought harm to the people whom such measures sought to benefit. Non-mutuality can result in exploitation, marginalization, powerlessness, cultural imperialism, and violence. Therefore, mutuality can enlighten us and encourage us to seriously consider the voices and the experiences of others in whatever good people seek to pursue. The intercultural community must be created mutually, must be co-constructed with all people.

Mutuality is rooted in Yoder's theology as well, especially when he writes about unity, ecumenism, true conversation, and binding and loosing.[55] Even in the concepts of the priesthood of all believers and the hermeneutic community, mutuality is already at work as an operative norm. However, it is crucial to explicitly highlight this norm, both because it contributes to the work of becoming an intercultural church, and because overlooking it could be detrimental, in that the regulative norm of mutuality helps to address power asymmetries and abuses. According to Calvin Redekop, throughout history, Mennonites have often "avoided and capitulated to the reality of power and its misuse in their corporate religious, communal, economic, familial, and gender relations."[56] By employing a better understanding of power dynamics and emphasizing mutuality, Mennonites can work together to confront all types of oppression and domination, and they can work to share power with all social groups so that all are fully welcomed and empowered. Sharing power mutually is connected to the ideals of respect, dignity of persons, and justice through equitable distribution of goods, as well as restorative and reconciliatory justice and love.

Mutuality also invites a broader conception of the church. While the mutuality advocated by the messianic community does not extend beyond the church setting, the theo-ethical norm of mutuality invites Mennonite churches to apply mutuality to groups outside of their own church and religious circles and to engage in more genuine conversation, working toward the construction of shared life together. In order to push Mennonite churches in this direction, Fernando Enns invites them to consider the church not only as the body of Christ but also as the *koinonia* based on a trinitarian foundation.[57] This model uses the example of the mutual indwelling of Father, Son, and Spirit, which "secures oneness in the midst of plurality, and yet, shields plurality from uniformist tendencies."[58] The model suggested by Enns invites Mennonite churches to seek mutual relationship with all humanity and the entirety of creation, based on theological imagining of how the Creator, the Son, and the Spirit relate mutually. This trinitarian understanding of mutuality also encourages Mennonites to seek justice, love, and shalom, and to do so mutually *with* others, and not merely *for* others. Mennonites are to be in a co-creative engagement *with* the other, rather than seeking a paternalistic *inclusion* of *those others*.

Because they are contextual and liberative in character, the above theo-ethical norms are not meant to constitute a fixed or comprehensive list applied homogeneously across all churches. There exist other norms that might be appropriate for MC Canada as it works to become intercultural. I chose these three examples in order to amplify particular features that this book has explored, features that resonate deeply with Mennonite perspectives and that offer clarity and insight for becoming an intercultural church. Furthermore, as examined in the preceding chapter, the Canadian context is always changing, and so the parameters for what I propose may be different twenty or even ten years from now. Yet the advantage of developing regulative theo-ethical norms is that they can be reinterpreted and corrected based on shifting social contexts and new theological insights.

6

Intercultural Mennonite Ecclesiology

While some churches are making more progress than others in becoming critically intercultural, none has yet fully reached that stage. Consequently, all churches are engaged in an ongoing journey. Throughout this journey, I am confident that God has provided us with glimpses or foretastes of what life-giving intercultural engagement can look like. Although these instances may not have become the norm yet, they inspire Mennonite churches to reimagine what it means to become truly intercultural. To illustrate this purpose, I share the experiences of Christen Kong, a social worker and member of the Toronto Chinese Mennonite Church who has witnessed and participated in life-giving intercultural engagements:

> At the Mennonite World Conference, I had the chance to meet Mennonites from around the world for the first time. What struck me most about these international gatherings was not just the geographical diversity, but, more importantly, the shared challenges and joys among their church communities, which mirrored those in Canada. Worshipping in different languages always stood out, as it exemplified the boundless reach of the Holy Spirit, transcending borders and boundaries.
>
> As I contemplated intercultural interactions, I initially envisioned the convergence of different racial groups. Yet, as I delved deeper, I realized it also encompassed intergenerational interactions. In our church, families spanning generations attend Mandarin, Cantonese, and English ministries, each with its distinct culture. For instance, the older generation comprises primarily first-generation Canadian immigrants, while the English-speaking

> members are second or third generation, expressing their faith differently. This intergenerational coexistence is a source of vitality, as it's not common for generations to meaningfully share the same space.
>
> At an MCEC gathering in Winnipeg, I was mentally preparing myself for an environment dominated by older white adults, as a significant portion of the Mennonite community fits this demographic. Although many Mennonite churches don't fall into this category, larger Mennonite gatherings tend to be quite homogeneous. That said, one of my most cherished moments occurred when a Japanese friend's mom approached me and greeted me. She expressed how much more at ease she felt upon spotting another Asian Mennonite in the crowd. I shared her sentiment. Even in that brief interaction, I felt acknowledged for my uniqueness, and it left a positive impact on her. It's these fleeting moments that truly make all the difference. Linked to the previous story, I firmly believe that healthy intercultural interactions aren't moments where I blend in because others don't know how to handle differences. Instead, they are the moments where differences are recognized, embraced, and welcomed into the space.
>
> One day, my friend from church, Elizabeth, hailing from Colombia, stumbled upon our church as we were worshipping on the front lawn. Intrigued, she inquired about our service and soon became a regular attendee. She has since moved back to Colombia, but what stands out is that many people hesitate to join our church because of its name – Toronto Chinese Mennonite Church – with an emphasis on "Chinese." Some have even asked if they can attend despite their non-Chinese background. However, Elizabeth's willingness to join without hesitation is truly heartwarming. She embraced Chinese cuisine every Sunday and loved it! When someone from a different culture can appreciate your culinary traditions, it brings about a deep sense of connection and vitality.[1]

Considering Christen's experience, we can glean the importance of celebrating both the commonalities and the differences among various groups. Her words also illustrate that life-giving intercultural interactions promote understanding, empathy, and connection across differences, enriching both individuals and communities. They underscore the significance of acknowledging and appreciating diversity and fostering inclusivity within various cultural contexts, be it through a simple gesture of greeting or in the grand scope of international gatherings that welcome people from diverse backgrounds.

This book comes to its high point by integrating the major topics that were covered in previous chapters. In light of shalom and the three theo-ethical norms that complement and enhance Mennonite ecclesiologies and traditions, this chapter develops specific ways of becoming an intercultural church in Canadian multicultural settler society. These can assist in shaping Canadian Mennonite practices through four sets of engagements: intercultural unity, radical discipleship and radical hospitality, shalom and prophetic dialogue in multicultural publics, and reconciliation and repentance in Indigenous-settler relations. Let us examine each in turn.

Intercultural Unity

In the Anabaptist-Mennonite tradition, through baptism one repents, is cleansed of one's sins, and joins an alternative community where all who are baptized wholeheartedly accept the lordship of Jesus Christ and follow his new way of life. This baptism also consists of the baptism of blood, signifying that one is willing to accept any suffering and sacrifice that comes as a result of following Jesus and loving others, even our enemies. Since all the people who join this alternative community are brothers and sisters in Christ, Christians are called to love one another and work for unity. As the church works for this unity, followers are asked to give up their old ways of life and renounce pride and self-centredness.

To live toward this new creation, theologians like Yoder and Larry Miller argue for becoming a transcultural church community based on the fact that in Christ, there is no longer Jew or Greek, enslaved or free person, male or female, rich or poor, or white or Black.[2] Yet this view can mislead, as if to say that one's social location, gender, or ethnocultural or racial identity is no longer important. This is dangerous, as I argued in chapter 5, because it can lead to claims of racial colour-blindness and cause us to ignore imbalanced power dynamics within our communities. In other words, in a Mennonite church where the "ethnic" Mennonites form the dominant group, this belief may implicitly support regimes of whiteness while pressuring people who do not adhere to this norm to assimilate to the dominant group and to dismiss the issues of ethnicity and race. It may even silence marginalized critical voices by treating difference as inconsequential – thereby upholding the status quo. From a contextual liberative theological perspective informed by the theo-ethical norm of mutuality, Mennonite churches must be attentive to social location and ethnocultural identities and analyze existing power dynamics within the church community.

Being part of the new creation does not mean overlooking our social locations and ethnocultural realities; rather, it entails giving up the old ways of life that utilized and manipulated these identities, and which were therefore complicit in violence, oppression, and injustice. As believers incorporate these realities, the church commits to working toward new relationships free from violence and oppression, and in which people from all backgrounds and social locations are loved, treated justly, and empowered to thrive. This involves the full participation of all members of the church body, so that no one is left out and everyone contributes to communal life.

The work of unity, as Yoder writes, is not merely an acknowledgment of people from different backgrounds, or simply a matter of trying to find a common denominator among different groups of people.[3] Rather, it involves working toward an authentic unity in which everyone strives for mutual interaction and transformation. This work of unity is not simply a secondary task – it is the very nature and core calling of the people who have been baptized and who commit to follow Jesus. Seen in this light, the Anabaptist-Mennonite understanding of baptism invites intercultural unity: unity sought in a manner that takes seriously ethnic, gender, racial, socio-economic, and other backgrounds, and that does not require people from different backgrounds to conform or assimilate.

How, then, are Mennonites called to work toward this intercultural unity in a situation where Mennonite ethnicity has been the dominant ethnicity and white people have been the dominant racial group? I will first focus on Mennonite ethnicity before examining Mennonite whiteness. Since ethnic character and identity markers are fluid across time, as explained in chapter 3, it is first of all important to recognize that Mennonite ethnic markers are subject to continuous change. This is a normal process, even an inevitable one. Thus, there is no need, at least for the dominant ethnic group,[4] to fear changes in ethnic identity or to attempt to strictly maintain their ethnic boundaries and exclude other ethnic communities. Acknowledging a diversity of cultural and ethnic groups within Mennonite identity can help our churches move from being monocultural to intercultural communities. Instead of having churches centred around those of Dutch, Russian, Swiss, and/or German background, they should embrace the many different groups that exist in our rich and diverse Mennonite churches; together, without one single group dominating, we can strive to mutually construct Mennonite identity and peoplehood.

In chapter 2, I provided a diagram that depicts the current composition of Mennonite peoplehood (figure 2.1). It shows that faith is the largest identity factor and that the boundary around it is porous enough that anyone who commits to the Mennonite faith can join. At the same time, there is a Mennonite culture, which is shaped and informed by Mennonite faith and ethnicity. Then, there is the ethnic aspect, by which I mean those of Russian, Swiss, German, and Dutch background. Even though this is the smallest facet of identity, it is still significant. This is the circle that is impermeable to outsiders. A healthy intercultural Mennonite community, of the type I am advocating, is visualized in figure 6.1.

As the church centres faith and embraces it as the foundational identity factor, it also celebrates several cultures and ethnicities that are part of the community and that inform and shape the church's identity, vision, mission, theologies, structures, and policies. The church will continue to recognize the special contributions of Swiss, German, Dutch, and Russian Mennonites, who will remain as the largest ethnic groups. Yet, they will be considered one important part of the community among others, rather than the dominant group.

In guiding the churches from the current understanding of Mennonite peoplehood toward the construction of an interethnic church, on a practical level, I find the "Continuum for Moving from Monocultural to Intercultural" useful. I also find the differences between ethnic theology and ethnotheology, as articulated by Charles Kraft, quite helpful. On a practical level, the continuum outlines six different stages: denial of difference, defence against difference, minimization of difference, acceptance of difference, adaptation to difference, and integration of difference.[5] Local churches within MC Canada are at different stages in

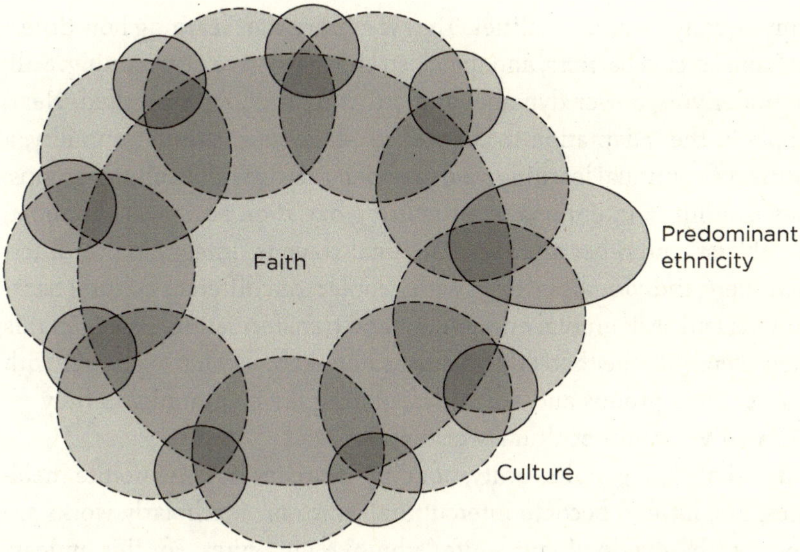

Figure 6.1 | A complex Venn diagram representing the structure of the intercultural Mennonite Church, where faith is at the core, intersecting with multiple overlapping circles that symbolize the diversity of cultures (mid-sized circles) and ethnicities (smallest circles), with the predominant ethnicity represented by the largest among the ethnic circles.

this continuum, but the most important point is that they be willing to move toward the next stage. In brief, people in the "denial of difference" stage believe that their culture is the only "real" one, and so they create institutions and policies that exclude those who stand against them. Individuals in "defence against difference" stage think that their culture is the best way to live. Consequently, they may create institutions with limited tolerance of people from different ethnocultural backgrounds, but mostly they maintain their dominant power and privilege through their formal policies, practices, teachings, and decision making. Next, there is the "minimization of difference." Folks at this stage recognize a diversity of food, customs, and traditions, but they assume that their values, truths, and needs are universal. As a result, they make official diversity policies and statements and attempt to be inclusive by recruiting diverse staff members and workers; however, they do not make any changes in culture, policies, and decision making. Those who are in the "acceptance of difference" stage recognize that their own culture contains many equally complex realities. They therefore start learning how different "isms" create barriers, and they also engage in diversity training. Still, the underlying power dynamic and structure are left untouched. Next, people in the "adaptation to difference" stage have cultural humility, a posture of continual learning, and are open tow different cultural groups. They commit to intentional restructuring based on anti-racist, feminist, anti-ableist, and other analyses. The final stage is "integration of difference": here, individuals interact with people from different cultural backgrounds and seek mutual enrichment and transformation. People in this stage exemplify the theo-ethical norms noted above, sharing power with other cultural groups and mutually building the community to fully reflect all diverse ethnocultural world views.

In striving for genuine unity, not only churches but Mennonite theologies, too, have to become intercultural, since most scholarly works are produced by the dominant white "ethnic" Mennonites. For this endeavour, Christian anthropologist Charles Kraft offers helpful guidance. According to Kraft, *ethnography* is the description of a particular culture, while *ethnology* is the understanding of "culture in general on the basis of comparison and analyses of data from many cultures."[6] Based on these concepts, Kraft has developed the terms "ethnic theology" and "ethnotheology." Ethnic theology is a theology that emerges within a particular framework for interpreting reality, such as a Western, Asian, or African world view. Ethnotheology, by contrast, is a theology that is developed by comparing insights from different ethnic theologies, and that seeks to discover commonality and difference so as to construct new theological insights. Recognizing the distinction between these two concepts allows us to situate Mennonite theologies. When examining Mennonite theologies taught in theological institutions, it is evident that most of these theological perspectives are Western ethnic theologies. Understanding that fact, it is important to reflect on how ethnic theologies can become more ethnotheological – or, to put it differently, intercultural.

Based on this, and in light of our understanding of theo-ethical norms, I propose four practical ways by which Mennonite theologies can become more intercultural and unified at the same time. First, as I discussed in chapter 3, we need to recognize more fully that all Mennonite theologies are profoundly contextual. Second, we must encourage "non-ethnic" Mennonites to reinterpret sources of theology that white "ethnic" Mennonites have utilized to construct their dominant theologies, such as historical documents from the sixteenth century. The interpretations of "non-ethnic" Mennonites can provide new insights and understandings of Mennonite theologies because they may perceive some important aspects that white Mennonite theologians have failed to emphasize, like the role of the Holy Spirit and the importance of solidarity. Third, we must reach out to new dialogue partners within the wider Mennonite community, especially theologians from different cultural contexts. This includes theologians from the Global South, but also those working in Northern America who have been relegated to the edges of our traditional theological dialogue (e.g., those from Indigenous, African Canadian, Asian Canadian, and other communities). Fourth, we must have greater recognition and accord more value to theological differences that emerge from different ethnocultural contexts. One way of doing this while also engaging with one another is through global theological flows that are transculturally shared, such as liberation, feminism, ecology, human rights, and peace/reconciliation.[7]

White Mennonites can start working for intercultural unity by continually acknowledging their whiteness and understanding how they are benefiting from white privilege. Observing how Mennonites in North America in the late nineteenth and early twentieth centuries became part of white identity and participated in the othering of Black communities, Canadian Mennonite sociologist Timothy Epp asserts that white Mennonites "must begin to acknowledge the ways by which we have contributed to the suffering of racialized populations and to recognize their truths. In addition ... we also need to acknowledge lines of power running through our relationships, and that we have often placed ourselves on the side of the oppressor."[8] This recognition is crucial for Epp because, without properly examining the past, there can be no constructive and healthy progress between white and BIPOC Mennonites.

As white Mennonites work to recognize their past and present, they can also seek to overcome the six approaches identified by Tobin Miller mentioned in chapter 5. One practical way to help white Mennonites interrogate their own whiteness is by actively seeking out and committing to conversation and building relationships with Christians who are not white, rather than staying within their own dominant white community. Malinda Berry recognizes that Mennonites have been actively involved in ecumenical and interfaith dialogues, but she points out at these dialogues were conducted among predominantly white communities.[9]

In 2013, a respected organization called the Public Religion Research Institute did a study in the United States that exposed an important aspect of modern segregation. It shows that the friendship networks of white Americans are 91 per cent white, and that 75 per cent of white Americans do not have a single racialized friend. Here, "friend" is defined as someone within one's inner circle, beyond just colleagues, classmates, church members, or neighbours. To see how this dynamic had changed over the course of a decade, the institute did another study in 2022. They discovered that the friendship networks of white Americans remained the same, around 90 per cent white; but, the number of people in the category of "not knowing a single racialized friend" had decreased from 75 per cent to 67 per cent.[10] Still, this research shows the considerable segregation between white and racialized people. No wonder so many white Americans do not understand racism and the challenges and oppressions that racialized people experience every day!

A comparable study was conducted by Statistics Canada in 2013. It revealed that 94 per cent of white Canadians belonged to friendship networks that consisted exclusively of individuals from their own racial background.[11] Although further research is currently lacking, the prevailing trend in the United States suggests that Canada might face a similar pattern. Furthermore, Statistics Canada has observed that this inclination toward homogeneity in friendship networks is even more pronounced within religious contexts, particularly when a religious group closely aligns itself with a specific ethnic community, as is the case with Canadian Mennonites. Consequently, it is fair to assert that there exists a significant degree of segregation between white Mennonites and racialized individuals.

These studies underscore the vital importance of deliberate efforts to relate to racialized groups, foster relationship, and engage collectively in the pursuit of racial justice. It is essential to recognize that not all non-white groups or individuals face identical levels of marginalization; indeed, the distribution of privilege can vary, as highlighted by an intersectional perspective. This mutual endeavour should encompass shared participation and leadership, ensuring adequate representation for all ethnocultural and racial groups. The church must actively encourage local congregations to stand in solidarity with racialized communities and demand justice, rather than merely issuing statements like the ones released by the MC USA executive board on 1 June 2020, following the murder of George Floyd,[12] or the statement from the executive staff group of MC Canada calling for a time of prayer and lament over social injustice.[13] To achieve true intercultural unity, it is imperative that we address and name white domination and privilege within the church while standing in solidarity with racialized communities and advocating for justice in the public sphere.

At the same time, racialized Mennonite church members must themselves engage in critical reflection. It is common for predominantly racialized Canadian churches, particularly those attended by first-generation immigrants, to hold patriarchal views and to harbour biases against queer individuals, an issue that extends beyond Mennonite circles and is prevalent in other denominations as well. We must bring an intersectional lens to bear on this issue because, on occasion, racialized members can inflict harm and engage in exclusionary practices. Therefore, it is essential that churches recognize how racialized individuals may perpetuate other forms of exclusion. Like white Mennonites, racialized Mennonites, their unique "glory and honour" notwithstanding, are capable of engaging in negative practices that need to be identified and abandoned.

Radical Discipleship and Radical Hospitality

Another concrete way of becoming an intercultural church is by practising radical hospitality, which connects with theo-ethical norms, and by following the example of God, who offers radical welcome to all living beings, desiring the full restoration of all creation. This theological framework of welcome or hospitality is deeply related to Anabaptist-Mennonite understandings of communion. In Anabaptist-Mennonite traditions, the Lord's Supper is generally viewed as a reminder that Christians are partaking in the life, teaching, and ministry of Jesus and recommitting to the vow that the believers took when they were baptized. This also means that, as followers of Christ, Christians are called to live in harmony with other church members. Recommitting to accepting the lordship of Jesus and following his teachings means choosing to live out radical discipleship and, if necessary, even to give up one's life for this calling. Since this is a robust commitment, Mennonites do not expect everyone will make this choice. Accordingly, communion has been traditionally reserved for people who exhibit such strong dedication. For this reason, some Mennonite churches do not offer communion to those who have not been baptized or who are not willing to make the full commitment.

However, Jesus's redemptive work was not merely for the disciples – it was for the whole world. In his ministry, Jesus ate and had fellowship with outcasts, the poor, and "sinners." Consequently, after observing the meal encounters of Jesus, John Rempel, a Canadian theologian, asserts that Jesus was wildly inclusive.[14] He states that the decisive factor determining who can join the table "is not being an insider or outsider but being willing to be changed. In my view, there is room at the table for unbaptized people who are drawn to the company of Jesus and his friends. Accepting the offer of grace implies a decision, not agreement on the contentious theological and sexual questions of the day, but a decision for Christ."[15] Eleanor Kreider also argues that, from the perspective of Mennonite tradition, it is important to maintain a productive tension between open and closed fellowship, grace and sanctity, inclusion and boundary.[16]

Informed by this understanding of communion, believers can practise radical hospitality with those who are already baptized and can make changes in church policies, cultures, theologies, and systems so that all members from different backgrounds are fully included. At the same time, since radical hospitality must by definition go beyond our own community, believers have a duty to welcome non-members and those who, while perhaps not committed, are open to receiving the gifts and welcome offered to them. Unquestionably, that welcome will look different from that which is extended to those within the inner circle, those who are baptized.

Within the inner circle, communion can be emphasized as our robust commitment to discipleship, but to the outer circle, table fellowship can be emphasized as a welcoming invitation to all. Alan and Eleanor Kreider assert that from "bounded set" table fellowship, Mennonite churches can move to the "centred set" and even to an "open set," depending on each local context.[17] The "bounded set" approach to communion draws a strict line between insiders and outsiders, and only those who are baptized can partake in table fellowship. The "centred set" approach welcomes non-baptized people to join in table fellowship – but only those who are committed to embrace the core convictions of Christian faith. Hence, for this approach, communion can be utilized as a pathway to baptism for non-baptized people. The "open set" approach emphasizes the importance of inclusivity and so welcomes anyone to join in table fellowship, even those who are not committed. This has implications for how we reimagine mission (as I show below). Although "open set" communion can be used to invite people to be baptized, it does not stress baptism as much as the "centred set" approach does. Whatever approach to table fellowship is chosen, all emphasize some aspects of openness and some aspects of closedness, because saying "yes" to some convictions means saying "no" to others. For example, saying "yes" to radical hospitality and its correlates – justice, love, and peace – means saying "no" to racism, white supremacy, oppression, injustice, and hatred. This entails a critical discernment of which aspects of openness to embrace.

Another possibility for communion that Eleanor Kreider proposes is to have many types of table fellowship, from generously open meals to bounded ceremonial ones. She offers eight forms of eucharistic fellowships that a church can implement.[18] Within a Mennonite understanding of communion, this means that each church (as well as the larger Mennonite Church) can create a culture, environment, and structures that are welcoming and respectful, are willing to change, and are always open to hear the thoughts and views of diverse people, regardless of whether they are people in the inner circle. Through constant dialogue and engagement, churches can cultivate a willingness to be transformed as well, since through the Spirit, God can work through non-believers. As the welcomed guests, non-believers can bring gifts and blessings that surprise us as the presence of God. Moreover, believers are witnessing to the world of what intercultural community looks like – by living in a unity grounded in the love of God that communion symbolizes, and by becoming a radically welcoming church. Through radical discipleship, members are even witnessing to the world God's desire for humans to be called to live out their diversity and differences.

The radical hospitality that is expressed through the practice of communion by Mennonites and the norm of hospitality can be framed as "radical welcome," an expression coined by Stephanie Spellers. She states that radical welcome is "first and foremost a spiritual practice. It combines the Christian ministry of welcome and hospitality with a faithful commitment to doing the theology, spirituality, and *systemic* work to eliminate historic, systemic barriers that limit the genuine embrace of groups generally marginalized in mainline churches."[19] Spellers explains more specifically how a church can authentically be hospitable and welcoming. She differentiates between inviting, inclusive, and radical welcome churches. An inviting church invites people who have different backgrounds but requires them to assimilate to the church's existing culture and practices and to adopt the dominant identity of the congregation. An inclusive church takes more seriously its responsibility to incorporate marginalized groups, and so it makes statements and preaches about the importance of being an inclusive congregation. It sees the need to embrace others. Nonetheless, the effort to effect change is mostly focused on an individual level and does not examine closely how the church system and its prevailing power dynamics are structured. By contrast, a "radical welcome church" seeks a truly mutual relationship with different groups. It perceives others as gifts from God and wants the church to express the full range of voices within the congregation. In order to make this a reality, such a church makes an intentional effort to invite and welcome people and include those from the margins. It also shares power so that, together; all can shape the church's identity, mission, and leadership in mutual respect. Spellers asserts that a radical welcome church also seeks mutually transforming relationships with its surrounding neighborhoods and struggles together to overcome all forms of social oppression.[20]

A radical welcome framework can serve to identify who are the "others" in our local church, who are in positions of power, how power is structured in a church, and how to transform the culture, leadership, and dominant system of the church. It strives to go beyond invitation and inclusion. Spellers defines "others" as any groups that are "likely to experience patterns of historic, systemic oppression and marginalization in your congregation and/or denomination, especially given your church's dominant race, culture, language, generation, socioeconomic class, educational level, sexual orientation and physical ability."[21] In other words, they have been subjected to processes of "othering"; thus "others" are created rather than simply found. As I argued earlier, "ethnic" Mennonite churches predominantly maintain white male heteronormativity; as a result, in Northern America, Mennonites who do not speak English, who did not grow up in a traditional Mennonite family, people of colour, women, and LGBTQAI2+ people are marginalized. Thus, it is important for Mennonite churches to practise a more robust welcome and to adopt practices of mutuality to change the church throughout – its norms, structures, policies, culture, and theological perspective. Through this effort, the radical welcome framework claims that not only will the other find a welcoming space in the church, but the dominant group will also finally be "free to embrace and be transformed by authentic relationship with the margins."[22] This framework does not seek to dismiss Mennonite traditions; rather, it aims to build on core faith values and to empower practices that allow us to concretely live out a Mennonite ecclesial vision that accounts for intercultural realities, this is sensitive to power dynamics, and that works mutually with marginalized people.

Shalom and Prophetic Dialogue in Multicultural Publics

As I discussed in chapter 2, from the beginning of their movement, Mennonites have engaged in missionary efforts. Yet, what would missions look like if Mennonites embraced more fully the theo-ethical norms of mutuality and hospitality? For Christians, historically and traditionally, mission was generally viewed as a one-way communication in which the messengers of the gospel shared the gospel with non-believers; however, current missiologists advocate for a more dialogical approach. Developing this idea further, Stephen Bevans and Roger Schroeder offer a new approach to mission called prophetic dialogue.[23] Bevans, with another scholar, Cathy Ross, recognizes that this specific term is not found in the Bible, but the approach is nevertheless implicit "in the best missiological thinking and practice of the past."[24] The idea is to maintain the tension between dialogue and prophetic speaking; it indicates that on some occasions, emphasis should be given to dialogue, and on other occasions, to prophetic speaking.

According to Ross and Bevans, mission as dialogue first means that it is not a monologue, and neither does it proceed from paternalistic gestures toward "others" from whom nothing can be learned.[25] At the same time, mission as prophecy means sharing the good news of the kingdom of God through our lives, actions, and words.[26] This presumes having something to share, which is the root of authentic missional work. In light of the message of justice and peace in the Bible, Christians are called to speak the truth and to oppose any kind of violence, injustice, oppression, and idolatry, and to offer hope in hopeless situations. However, Christians can denounce violence and injustice only when they are in solidarity with marginalized communities and are aware of the poverty and oppression experienced by these communities. Moreover, since relationship "with" is key to mutuality, Christians also need to be in a position to learn and receive from non-Christians – and through this engagement, to learn about God and the world in a much deeper and broader way. Relationship "with" also prescribes that power be shared fairly and respectfully. Hence, missional work requires Christians to be mindful of their power and privilege and to engage in a non-paternalistic way with those in dialogue.

In light of prophetic dialogue, Mennonite churches in Canada have opportunities for engaging in missional work in new ways. This is not to assert that Mennonites have not been involved in dialogue or that prophetic elements are not found in Mennonites' missional work. As explored in chapter 2, examples of this approach can be seen in Mennonites' mission agencies and social services, like MCC. Still, a more adequate and full engagement in missional work would enhance Mennonite intercultural practices. From a contextual and liberative perspective, missional work needs to consider the social, ethnocultural, spiritual, and economic dimensions of society, and to participate in the holistic task of liberating marginalized people from all kinds of oppression. Seeing this holistic understanding of missional work through an Anabaptist-Mennonite lens, Mennonite churches are called not only to share the gospel of peace, send missionaries, and plant churches, but also to more fully participate in the work for shalom, which encompasses all areas of human life. This entails standing against racism, sexism, oppressive ideologies, and being in solidarity with the weak and the marginalized. It entails fighting against hunger and poverty and working for the social welfare of all people. In this endeavour, as I have explained in chapter 4, it is crucial to cultivate *convivencia* or shalom as alternatives to structural and cultural violence. Before examining more deeply how shalom should be created, I will explain what structural and cultural violence are and how they are intrinsically related.

Johann Galtung differentiates between three types of violence: direct, structural, and cultural. He explains that the cause of direct violence is often linked to structural violence and justified by cultural violence. Like the tip of an iceberg, direct violence is visible, but structural and cultural violence are hidden underneath, and so they are hard to identify. This threefold paradigm of violence helps to demonstrate that shalom involves action against structural violence and cultural violence.[27]

Social structure is a social arrangement of human relationships on various levels, from the macro to the micro, in which institutions, social norms, and value systems are interconnected. The national economy, social classes, educational systems, family, religion, and legal and political systems are all part of the social structure. They influence and shape people's identities, interests, and interactions, and they can either limit or advance people's actions and decisions. Since people depend on social structures, they are pivotal for their safety and well-being; but, unfortunately, some social structures cause violence, like institutionalized racism and ethnocentrism, as was discussed in chapter 3. Structural violence "refers to the physical, psychological, and spiritual harm that certain groups of people experience as a result of the unequal distribution of power and privilege ... Structural violence degrades, dehumanizes, damages, and kills people by limiting or preventing their access to the necessities of life or for its flourishing."[28] And just as white people have a hard time perceiving their white privilege, it is hard to identify and name structural sins that exist in modern society, because to the people in power, these systems are seen as part of life, even "necessary." If these systems are not identified, they will continue to oppress people from generation to generation.

Therefore, in the work of shalom, one of the roles of the churches is to unmask and reveal violent structures that exist in society, challenge them, and discern carefully if they are complicit in them. After discerning and challenging structural violence, the next step is transforming these practices into systems that create and sustain peace: creating structures and systems that protect the weak and the environment, that treat people with respect, that offer equal distribution of power and privilege, and that strive for the flourishing of each person and community.

Galtung asserts that in order to dismantle structural violence, cultural violence needs to be challenged as well, because cultural violence justifies and even legitimizes direct and structural violence.[29] The stereotype that Latinos are lazy, that all Muslims are terrorists, or that men are superior to women are some examples of cultural violence. Such ideologies and attitudes circulate in language and biases and become embodied in systems and behaviours. To challenge cultural violence, it is necessary to identify and name distorted beliefs and ideologies. This happens through critical thinking and by being in solidarity with marginalized communities. Hearing the voices of minoritized people is crucial since it opens up possibilities for the dominant group to see the kinds of oppression and violence that minorities experience. In Canada, where Christianity historically has been the dominant religion, it is crucial for Christians to hear what kind of injustice and inequality people from other religions experience. Moreover, society remains male-dominated. That reality has ramifications, especially for those of us who are male and desire justice. Hence, men continually need to hear what women experience, and they must work to challenge cultural violence and create shalom, in which everyone is welcomed, loved, and treated justly. We must do this work mutually. This is the shalom and *convivencia* that intercultural Mennonite churches are called to pursue.

Reconciliation and Repentance in a Settler Society

Reconciliation is one of the core callings of discipleship for Mennonites. It is understood as a lifelong journey that consist of several steps, including recognition of wrong, repentance, taking responsibility, receiving forgiveness, making amends, and restoring trust. This work of reconciliation can only begin by situating it in a specific socio-historical context and repenting for one's concrete wrongdoings and sins. Inspired by this calling, Mennonites have developed several healthy approaches to conflict and mediation.

In a context in which churches have committed injustices and have subsequently been silent, the work of reconciliation is imperative from an Anabaptist-Mennonite perspective. Yet, it is important to listen to the criticism that reconciliation is a largely white agenda. Jennifer Harvey explains that in racial justice work, reconciliation seeks to overcome white supremacy and the deep racial divide through "a universalist ethic that emphasizes the humanity we all share and need to honor more deeply. Interracial togetherness becomes the solution to the problem of division."[30] Such an understanding focuses primarily on creating more authentic relationships among different racial groups, but it can too easily ignore the actual reality of broken relationships, which has deep historical roots, and the structural violence that perpetuates these divisions. Instead, Christians could consider using the framework of reparation. Unlike reconciliation, the reparation framework is premised on a particularistic ethic that acknowledges real racial differences as "the only places from and through which we can and must begin to understand and reconfigure our relationships to one another. It insists that our differences are a result of a history we share, one that puts us in intimate relationship with one another."[31] Hence, starting from the position of racial difference, reparative racial justice work examines unredressed histories and social structures that continue to alienate and harm racialized communities and unjustly benefit white communities.

I recognize that if reconciliation is not situated in a specific history and context, it can become vague, idealized, and even a means to ignore the suffering and injustice that marginalized communities have experienced. This approach has the tendency to move too quickly to a new relationship, as if the past has been resolved. Yet, when Harvey problematizes reconciliation, she is predominantly focusing on the issue of racism between white and Black people in the United States; so far, there has not been any official process to resolve this issue in the American context. In Canada, as well, there has not been any official process for dealing with racism; however, in the context of relations between white settlers and Indigenous people, an official process has been called forth by the Truth and Reconciliation Commission of Canada (TRC). Through this endeavour, repressed truths were spoken, violence done against Indigenous communities was acknowledged, and some work of repentance followed from the government and a few major church denominations. Although the TRC does not go far enough in holding the government or those individuals who perpetrated violence and embodied genocidal attitudes and actions accountable, I believe that reconciliation is an appropriate framework, at least within the issues related to white settlers and Indigenous communities. Still, as the Honourable Steven Point argues, reconciliation can only happen when white settlers accept their wrongdoings and take responsibility by stopping the destruction of Indigenous land and the many deaths of Indigenous women and girls.[32] Thus, it is important not to speak as if reconciliation has been accomplished, or to assume that it can be done quickly so that Canadians can arrive at a point at which simply move on. Being informed by Indigenous voices and experiences, the TRC states that reconciliation must become a way of life for all people living in Canada. Reconciliation requires not only "apologies, reparations, the relearning of Canada's national history, and public commemoration, but also ... real social, political, and economic change."[33]

The fact that Mennonite churches are predominantly white and have benefited from settler colonialism and the systems that it props up creates opportunities for repentance in the work of reconciliation. Specifically, churches can begin the work of repentance by recognizing how they have been complicit with colonial and white supremacist social structures, how they have benefited from various types of oppression, and how they have remained silent or ignorant in the face of the injustice that occurred on this land, as discussed in chapter 4. To be sure, Christian churches in Canada have been participating in some acts of repentance toward Indigenous communities; but I am also advocating here for repentance from racism, ethnocentrism, sexism, and other forms of injustice.

Jeremy Bergen, a Canadian Mennonite theologian, offers some examples of how a church can repent. He explains that ecclesial repentance means that "the past cannot be undone and that an apology is deeply inadequate. Nevertheless, an apology imagines a way forward. An apology ought to acknowledge the moral violation, the harm caused, and the inability of confession to repair the damage, and thus place the community before the mercy of God and human victims in the fragile hope of a reconciled future."[34] As Bergen rightly asserts, while repentance itself may not be enough, it is the very first action to take if the church wants to engage with people who have been hurt by it. Bergen then offers a detailed picture of how ecclesial repentance entails "confession of sin, public acknowledgment, commitment to a future, and public witness."[35] Repentance is not only a matter of feeling badly about what one has done; it is an ongoing commitment that requires the perpetrator to publicly state his or her wrongdoings in order for the victims to know that the perpetrator has acknowledged his or her sin. It is more than a simple claim that one is sorry; it involves ongoing work for reparation and the rebuilding of trust so that one can engage with victims in the future. This is necessary because an "act of repentance is as much or more about the future as it is about the past."[36] Repentance needs to happen not only to solve past problems, but also to determine how fractured parties can live together in the future. Of course, ecclesial repentance does not guarantee that victims will be healed and that everyone will get along together, but it is the first concrete step for the church to take – and necessary if we are to see how God and the victims will respond to it.

Starting from ecclesial repentance, Mennonite churches must come up with a new way of living and relating on this land. As they engage with Indigenous and other racialized people in the work of reconciliation, the norm of mutuality can serve an aspirational role in the ongoing work for a future in which all people can live together, in *convivencia*, in peace and justice. Since this work aims to live out a reality that does not presently exist, it requires a moral imagination that evokes people's "reason, sensing, judgement, understanding[, and] conscience," and the will to "seek and create spaces beyond the places that exist" without being confined by our current reality.[37] Rather than being a utopic fantasy, moral imagination is, as John Paul Lederach describes it, the capacity to imagine something rooted in the real challenges that people are going through. It entails "giving birth to that which does not yet exist ... [It] is the capacity to imagine and generate constructive responses and initiatives that, while rooted in the day-to-day challenges of violence, transcend and ultimately break the grips of those destructive patterns and cycles."[38]

One source of wisdom that may inform and inspire the moral imagination of Mennonite churches is the Indigenous understanding of belonging and co-living through treaty, a way of life that stands in stark contrast with a colonial and dominating way of existing. One specific treaty that the churches can explore is the Haudenosaunee Two Row Wampum (or Guswenta) Treaty, which was made by the Dutch and Haudenosaunee in the early 1600s. It was a treaty established for them and their future generations. Through this treaty, these two groups sought a mutual relationship. As they lived together in a single region, they did not dominate or interfere with each other; they respected each other's boundaries and the "middle row." At the same time, they were always in contact and actively shared spaces in a way that benefited and enriched both groups.[39] The treaty was symbolically recorded in a wampum belt featuring two purple rows: one representing the Dutch settlers' ships and the other representing the Haudenosaunee people's canoes, travelling side by side down the river of life without attempting to steer each other's vessels. This mutual relationship was founded on three core values, represented by three rows of white beads, each symbolizing a key principle. The first white row stands for a desire for peace and friendship; the second for respect; and the third for good intentions and the aim to establish a strong relationship. This historical example of *convivencia* between white settlers and Indigenous communities can offer inspiration as an intercultural model of engagement; as such it can give us hope that a new way of living is possible if all groups, particularly white Christians, are willing and committed. Reflecting on the Two Row Wampum Treaty and the work of reconciliation within Canada, Adrian Jacobs, the senior leader for Indigenous justice and reconciliation at the Christian Reformed Church, asserts that

> Four hundred and nine years ago Dutch and Haudenosaunee people were very different peoples: different languages, different technology, different clothing and ways, different ways of making decisions, different connections to creation, and different religions. And yet, we were able to establish a good relationship that lasted for some time. Today we are much closer than we were then: most of us speak the same English language, we live in the same Western world, go to the same schools, have the same governments over us, etc. Surely, we can have an even better relationship than we had at the beginning.[40]

While there is still so much work to do in this long journey of reconciliation, Jacobs is correct to believe that we are in a much better position and closer to each other than at anytime before.

Practising ecclesial repentance and incorporating the moral imagination embedded in the Guswenta Treaty, Mennonites are called to engage in the work of reconciliation on this land where treaties with Indigenous peoples have been broken. It is a positive sign that awareness is growing among Mennonite churches in Canada and the MCC, which recognize their historic complicity with policies and projects that contributed to the further marginalization of Indigenous communities and other people of colour. Furthermore, they are taking seriously the TRC's Calls to

Action. For example, across Canada, several Mennonite churches have supported Bill C-262, which demands that the government "enshrine the UN Declaration on the Rights of Indigenous Peoples into Canadian law."[41] Moreover, in 2020 the book *Be It Resolved: Anabaptists & Partner Coalitions Advocate for Indigenous Justice* was published by MCC Canada and MC Canada. It presents "a collection of over 90 documents detailing commitments Anabaptists have made to Indigenous justice and decolonization since the 1960s."[42] As the churches commit to continual engagement with the TRC Calls to Action and reparative work with Indigenous and racialized people, Mennonite theologians are required to theologize in a new way. This new theology needs to reflect the four theo-ethical norms examined throughout this chapter, which invite us to reimagine our relationships on this sacred land called Turtle Island. White Mennonites must justly and mutually engage with Indigenous communities and all other marginalized social groups, and they must commit to the work of reparation and reconciliation, all the while aiming toward shalom.

As I have discussed earlier, depending on one's context, interculturality can have different meanings. For this reason, it is crucial to situate any discussion about interculturality. In part 3 of this book, I have built upon a foundational principle of interculturality, shalom (explained in chapter 4), to ground the three theo-ethical norms in order to situate MC Canada as an intercultural church. As part of this process, from a contextual and liberative perspective (analyzed in chapter 3), it was necessary to identify excluding practices, power dynamics, and the matrix of oppression and privilege that exists within MC Canada. For this purpose, I have critically reassessed Mennonite peoplehood by analyzing sources, norms, and three Mennonite theologies – the messianic community, the missional church, and the shalom church – and I have identified some issues that prevent the church from becoming intercultural. Moreover, utilizing critical cultural and social theories, I have shown that people in the white "ethnic" Mennonite category are the dominant group, as well as how ethnic myopia and lax racial awareness have impeded the inclusion and integration of other social groups within the Mennonite community.

I then analyzed the "believed" and "experienced" church through various critical lenses to suggest how theo-ethical norms can be adequately and appropriately applied by Mennonites seeking to form an intercultural church in Canada. As a result, I suggested the following measures:

seeking intercultural unity; practising radical discipleship and radical hospitality; striving for shalom and prophetic dialogue in multicultural publics; and working for reconciliation in Indigenous-settler relations. These are the embodiments of fruitful intercultural engagement that reflect the theo-ethical norms of justice and love, hospitality, and mutuality – norms that are embedded in Mennonites' theologies, traditions, and praxes. They can serve to lead MC Canada toward a more contextual and liberative theology and praxis so that it can more faithfully live out its missional calling and the gospel of peace, with the ultimate goal of becoming a truly "transformed people" here in Canada.

CONCLUSION

In her 2022 book *The White Mosque: A Memoir*, Sofia Samatar, born to a Black Somali Muslim father and a white Swiss German Mennonite mother, shares her experience of trying to belong to a Mennonite community as someone who is not ethnically Mennonite:

> My friend was telling me that he still went to church, though he didn't believe in God. He went for tradition, community, mutual aid, and the chance to do activist work with like-minded people, because he believed in those things. He said the church was full of people like him. I thought this was awful. Going to church when you don't believe – doesn't this make a mockery of faith?
>
> My friend laughed. "I think you have a romantic idea of church." He was right. Today, he and I are part of the same congregation. It's a wonderful grab bag of singers and readers and prodigals and seekers, a miscellany of *either/or* and *both/end*. And today, if you ask me to name the strength of the Mennonite church, I would say it's precisely what looks like weakness and contradiction, the patchwork of people brought together in such different ways, by birth and faith and thirst, to build a house of effort and care. I would say our strength is that we can't get everyone on the same page. I would say my church almost looks like my idea of utopia. And I have to add that on a typical Sunday, with around 300 in attendance, you can count the people of color on your two hands.
>
> Ethnicity is a knot that's hard to sever. When I look at Mennonite communities, it seems clear that those who are joined by blood retain a means of attachment even if they no longer have faith. But those who are joined by faith can be detached by its

disappearance. I understand that someone like my father, deeply influenced by the Mennonite story, has no place in it any longer as a practicing Mennonite, unlike other non-practicing Mennonites who carry the banner of blood. But experience, just like blood, endures. How I wish this could be recognized, acknowledged, and celebrated, stories granted a status equal to that of DNA, perhaps even greater! It's the days spent together that make us part of each other. There is a genetics of storytelling, for stories too are encoded, inherited, lodged in the flesh.[1]

Samatar laments and yearns to see a day when Mennonites by faith will have their stories be considered and accepted as equal to or even greater than those stories told by ethnic Mennonites. Like Samatar, I and many other "half-Mennonites" are not saying that ethnic Mennonites have not been hospitable and welcoming to us. Ethnic Mennonites, in general, are marked by their practise of hospitality. The issue is that, in the church context, they continually identify themselves as the hosts and the "half-Mennonites" as "perpetual guests," people who are welcomed to stay but only within a certain boundary. While we preach that we are all God's family, sing that we are all welcomed, and participate in communion with a conviction that we are all part of the body of Christ, almost every aspect of community life is centred on Swiss, German, Dutch, and Russian Mennonites. The stories that are being told, the pictures that are being posted, the structure of worship, the content of sermons, the policies that are being made – they are all centred on the dominant group. Once a year, there might be an international potluck, intercultural worship service, or some kind of celebration of diversity, but all of these are limited to a certain space, place, and time. As a result, people like us do not feel that we can find full belonging. Echoing Samatar's words, hospitality is not enough, because as guests, no matter how kindly we are treated, we are "pressure[d] toward gratitude and conformity."[2] As members of the church community who are nonetheless viewed as "perpetual guests," we wonder: When can we share our stories of how we became Mennonites? When can we sing our songs that deeply touch our heart and spirit? And when can we hear someone who looks like us preach and utilize examples from our own cultural background? Often, we wonder if we should act and speak as active members of the church, or simply remain quiet and be grateful for what is being served to us. Will we ever be given a chance to practise mutual hospitality? After struggling with these issues for years, I write this book as a way to move forward and to offer concrete recommendations for how we can build a community in which "half-Mennonites" can experience full belonging with ethnic Mennonites.

In MC Canada, where white Mennonites from Swiss, German, Dutch, and Russian ethnicities form the dominant group, and in a social context where ethnocultural and racial differences are being managed and controlled by way of traditional Canadian understandings of multiculturalism, becoming a critical intercultural church is a faithful way for Mennonites to live out discipleship, their own historic peace church tradition, and their missional identity in Canada. Particularly in this multicultural society, it means to be both a decolonizing and anti-racist community. I have used an interdisciplinary approach to bolster this claim. Through descriptive, critical, and constructive analyses, which I referred to as a *contextual liberative approach*, I briefly examined Canadian Mennonites' history, beliefs, and social dynamics. I incorporated critical social theories and cultural theologies to interrogate the existing power dynamics, dominant ideologies, cultural imperialism, and unjust social structures embedded in Canadian Mennonite communities. These lenses and analyses helped to explain why some experiences and voices are more valued than others and what is necessary for a more robust consideration of the perspectives and voices of marginalized people.

Chapter 1 examined the "believed church" (the church as a theological reality), particularly three different Mennonite ecclesiological approaches – the messianic church, the missional church, and the shalom church. These theological ideals, widely accepted by Mennonites, show that Mennonites aspire to engage with the world, engage in dialogue with those who hold different theological views and with people from diverse ethnocultural backgrounds, work toward reconciliation, seek peace, and strive for social transformation. These commitments, beliefs, and aspirations are not only crucial aspects of interculturality but are also distinctive Mennonite ways of becoming an intercultural church. By surveying the "experienced" church, in chapter 2, I showed that Mennonites have been actively engaging with the world, accommodating themselves to a drastically changing society without losing their Anabaptist-Mennonite traditions, and working to become a more global and diverse church. However, critical voices are raising issues of gender, race, and ethnicity and challenging the church to be more inclusive and welcoming so that it can be truly transformed and empowered to faithfully live out the gospel of peace.

To deepen the critical analysis of Mennonite peoplehood and to offer a constructive direction of how Canadian Mennonites can become intercultural, in chapter 3 I explored the contextual nature of theology and how faith, culture, ethnicity, and race inform and shape each other. Based on Stephen Bevans's six different models of contextual theology, I argued that the best of the Mennonite models can emerge through a contextual and liberative approach, which combines anthropological, praxis, and countercultural models. From the insights gleaned from cultural theologians and Canadian critical social theorists, in chapter 4 I interrogated Canadian multiculturalism and noted how it is built on the principles of white supremacy and settler colonialism, whereby white settlers control and manage ethnocultural and racial difference. In an effort to engage with difference in a more equitable, respectful, and mutual way, I sought to deepen the understanding of interculturality by briefly surveying different concepts of interculturality and formulating a foundational principle of interculturality from an Anabaptist-Mennonite perspective: that of shalom.

Chapter 5 began by critically reassessing Mennonite peoplehood from a contextual and liberative perspective to provide the material basis for particular guidelines on how Canadian Mennonite can become intercultural. Through reassessing the "believed" church, I identified five problematic issues in Mennonite peace theologies: (1) the sharp contrast between the church and the world; (2) the belief that Jesus and the Bible are the final authority, when, in reality, they rely on other theological sources without recognizing it; (3) a strong emphasis on Christology that dismisses the inclusive nature of God, Jesus, and the Holy Spirit; (4) assuming widely existing norms within the community, such as whiteness, patriarchy, and heteronormativity, which profoundly influence theological discourses; and (5) unconsciously assuming and being complicit in the colonial project. Furthermore, by reassessing the "experienced" church, building on chapter 2 and incorporating critical analysis of culture, race, and ethnicity from chapter 3, I argued that "ethnic myopia" and "lax racial awareness" are preventing the Mennonite community from constructing an anti-racist and intercultural church.

As a vehicle for naming, resisting, and transforming these exclusionary practices, I offered three theo-ethical norms, which are based on shalom as a foundational principle and Mennonite theology: justice and love, hospitality, and mutuality. These norms are interrelated, forming a kind of constellation through their various intersecting themes. The process of becoming an intercultural church is complex and multi-faceted, involving policy change and a reorientation of attitudes and actions. In this light, and because of the capacity of theological insights to inform Christians' actions and motivate change, in chapter 6 I focused on theo-ethical guidelines that may lead and empower churches within MC Canada to become intercultural. Through these theo-ethical norms, I encouraged Canadian Mennonite churches to seek intercultural unity and radical discipleship, which also requires radical hospitality, shalom through prophetic dialogue, and reconciliation and repentance.

Certainly, the theo-ethical norms I propose in this book are simply one way of encouraging Mennonite churches to become intercultural. As a male and immigrant scholar, I recognize my limited view, and so I welcome and encourage Mennonites from various social locations to write and speak about their own experiences of interculturality. Their voices will enrich the discourse on this topic. This particular intercultural project has focused on ethnocultural and racial difference. To deepen this work, other types of difference, such as gender, sexuality, age, and ability/disability, should also be considered.

Given our current context, all churches in Canada are called to engage with ethnocultural and racial difference. While this book has primarily focused on Mennonite churches in Canada, the theo-ethical norms and reflections on becoming an intercultural church I have offered here may benefit a wider circle of Christians from other traditions. This book will be especially helpful to Christian denominations that have dominant ethnic groups, like the Christian Reformed Church, the Presbyterian Church, the Anglican Church, the Lutheran Church, and others.

As MC Canada works to become an intercultural church, mutual and respectful interaction based on equity must occur between dominant and marginalized groups. Without this, there can be no genuine intercultural engagement. Moreover, people with the most power and resources must provide space for marginalized groups to thrive. They must also give up some of their privilege and power. Without this sacrifice and kenotic posture – a posture Jesus exemplified in Philippians 2:5–11 – equity cannot be established. At the same time, marginalized groups need to continually share their stories, be actively involved in leadership roles, and work to create belonging for all. They need to be empowered to engage in this transformative effort. This striving toward equity is profoundly biblical.

Luke 1:46–55 offers a well-known song of praise by Mary called the Magnificat. Once Mary learns that she will give birth to the Messiah, she tells us through this song what the Messiah will do. One of the tasks of this Messiah is to remove the powerful from their thrones and lift up the lowly. It depicts the crucial place that equity has in the Messiah's vision. In Luke 3, Luke cites a passage from Isaiah to describe John the Baptist. One of John's roles is to fill every valley and to make low every mountain and hill – in other words, to level the playing field. Luke is again telling us that equity is part of God's salvific work. The vision of equity, which is part of God's salvation, is also connected to the understanding of Jubilee. In Leviticus 25:1–13, God demands all people to be released from their debts, to free all slaves, and to return the land to those who owned it. Through Jubilee, God commands people with the most power and resources to make some sacrifice so that the poor and the enslaved can be empowered. When the crooked path is made straight, when the rough roads are made smooth, when the people with power sacrifice and the marginalized people are empowered, there will then be mutual, respectful, and intercultural interaction.

In becoming intercultural, "full Mennonites" would need to learn that God is the ultimate host of MC Canada. While they can be big sisters and brothers of this denominational family, they are not its mothers and fathers. At the same time, half-Mennonites are not perpetual guests – they are the family members of God. As a result, in this house, the practise of mutual hospitality is long overdue. It is about time to welcome half-Mennonites to serve as hosts, to empower them tell their stories, hang their pictures, move the furniture wherever they want, and fill the house with their sounds, smells, and dances. By making these changes, we transform our house into what Samatar describes as "an alien place."[3] The place will surely look, smell, and sound different; such changes, while sometimes messy, are nevertheless vital. For some ethnic Mennonites, witnessing these changes might cause a degree of anxiety, stress, and uneasiness because the house is not ordered and organized in the "Mennonite way." They might also experience some sense of loss because it is no longer "what it used to be." Nonetheless, by letting go of the need to control, they will experience the richness of this inter-ethnic and interracial family, the fullness of the body of Christ. Their world views will be broadened and their understanding of God will be deepened. Over time, the church will shift toward a new normal, one in which the glimpses of life-giving intercultural engagement offered throughout this book have become the norm.

NOTES

INTRODUCTION

1 "Canada in 2041: A Larger, More Diverse Population with Greater Differences between Regions," Statistics Canada, 8 September 2022, https://www150.statcan.gc.ca/n1/daily-quotidien/220908/dq220908a-eng.htm.

2 This is an expression used by T.D. Regehr in his analysis of Canadian Mennonites from 1939 to 1970. See Regehr, *Mennonites in Canada, 1939–1970: A People Transformed* (Toronto: University of Toronto, 1996).

3 Anabaptist-Mennonites have a long history of persecution. From 1525 and until the end of the sixteenth century, they were severely persecuted because of their religious convictions. It is estimated that five thousand Anabaptists were killed during this period. In the seventeenth century, Anabaptist-Mennonites were also persecuted by both Protestant and Catholic leaders in most of Europe. The book *Martyr's Mirror*, widely read in the Mennonite circle, preserves the memory of those persecuted during this period. Numerous Mennonites in Russia migrated to Canada between 1873 and 1884 seeking religious freedom and exemptions from military service. Another major wave of Russian Mennonites migrated to Canada to flee the new Communist government established in Russia in 1919. See "Who Are the Mennonites?," Mennonite Historical Society of Canada, accessed 22 September 2020, https://mhsc.ca/who-are-the-mennonites/.

4 See "Anabaptists around the World [2022]," Mennonite World Conference, accessed 11 June 2024, https://mwc-cmm.org/sites/default/files/featured-images/mwc_world_map_2022.png.

5 Conrad Kanagy, Elizabeth Miller, and John D. Roth, *Global Anabaptist Profile: Belief and Practice in Mennonite World Conference Churches* (Goshen, IN: Institute for the Study of Global Anabaptism, 2017), 29.

6 This is an expression that non-traditional Mennonites have used when they feel they are not fully included in Mennonite communities. Some people use it as a

way to express that they are not ethnically Mennonites, and others use it when they do not practise Mennonite faith. Other terms used are "segmented Mennonite" and "outsided Mennonite."

7 Royden Loewen, "The Poetics of Peoplehood: Ethnicity and Religion among Canada's Mennonites," in *Christianity and Ethnicity in Canada*, ed. Paul Bramadat and David Seljak (Toronto: University of Toronto Press, 2008), 348–57.

8 Paul Bramadat and David Seljak, "Charting the New Terrain: Christianity and Ethnicity in Canada," in *Christianity and Ethnicity in Canada*, ed. Paul Bramadat and David Seljak (Toronto: University of Toronto Press, 2008), 416–17.

9 *Canadian Oxford Dictionary*, 2nd ed. (2004), s.vv. "Multicultural" and "Intercultural."

10 Ted D. Regehr and Richard D. Thiessen, "Canada," *Global Anabaptist Mennonite Encyclopedia Online*, accessed 10 October 2023, https://gameo.org/index.php?title=Canada#Mennonites_in_Canada_Census_Figures.

PART ONE

1 Fernando Enns, "Believers Church Ecclesiology: A Vital Alternative within the Ecumenical Family," in *New Perspective in Believers Church Ecclesiology*, ed. Abe Dueck, Helmut Harder, and Karl Koop (Winnipeg: Canadian Mennonite University Press, 2010), 115.

2 While the distinction between the church as a theological reality and the church as a sociological reality may have begun much earlier, the earliest record can be found in Augustine of Hippo's *The City of God*, where he writes about the visible and the invisible church. See Justo González, *A History of Christian Thought*, vol. 2, *From Augustine to the Eve of the Reformation*, rev. ed. (Nashville, TN: Abingdon Press, 1987), 28. Later, this distinction was embraced somewhat differently by Zwingli and Calvin. Martin Luther also utilized this concept but named the distinction between the visible and the hidden church. See Fernando Enns, "Believers Church Ecclesiology: A Vital Alternative within the Ecumenical Family," in *New Perspectives in Believers Church Ecclesiology*, ed. Abe Dueck, Helmut Harder, and Karl Koop (Winnipeg: CMU Press, 2010), 110–11. Currently the Roman Catholic Church distinguishes between "sacrament" and "institution," between the "mystical body of Christ" and the "eucharistic body of Christ." See Douglas Bushman, "Introductions," in *The Sixteen Documents of Vatican II*, ed. Marianne Lorraine Trouvé (Boston: Pauline Books and Media, 1999). Gordon Kaufman, a Mennonite theologian, prefers to describe this distinction as that between eschatological and empirical speech about the church. See Gordon Kaufman, *Nonresistance and Responsibility: And Other Essays* (Newton, KS: Faith and Life Press, 1979), 56.

3 The term "Anabaptist-Mennonite" is used to encompass people who do align with Mennonite theological perspectives but who prefer not to be identified as Mennonites due to the strong ethnic and cultural connotations of the word. See Karl Koop, "Anabaptist and Mennonite Identity: Permeable Boundaries and Expanding Definitions," *Religion Compass* 8, no. 6 (2014): 199–207.

4 Gustavo Gutiérrez, *A Theology of Liberation*, rev. ed., trans. Sister Caridad Inda and John Eagleson (Maryknoll, NY: Orbis Books, 1988), xxxiv.

5 Frank Epp, *Mennonites in Canada, 1920–1940: A People's Struggle for Survival* (Toronto: Macmillan, 1982), 545.

6 Iris Marion Young, *Justice and the Politics of Difference* (Princeton, NJ: Princeton University Press, 1990), 171.

CHAPTER ONE

1 Due to the close relationship between peace theology and ecclesiology, as each type of peace theology is presented, the book explains how this particular view leads to a certain understanding of the church. The ten types of peace theologies are historic nonresistance, culturally engaged pacifism, social responsibility, apolitical nonresistance, the pacifism of the messianic community, radical pacifism, realist pacifism, Canadian pacifism, liberation pacifism, and neo-sectarian pacifism. See John Richard Burkholder and Barbara Nelson Gingerich, eds, *Mennonite Peace Theology: A Panorama of Types* (Akron, OH: Mennonite Central Committee Peace Office, 1991).

2 Duane Friesen, *Artists, Citizens, Philosophers: Seeking the Peace of the City* (Scottdale, PA: Herald Press, 2000).

3 Rachel Waltner Goossen, "'Defanging the Beast': Mennonite Responses to John Howard Yoder's Sexual Abuse," *Mennonite Quarterly Review* 89, no. 1 (2015): 7–80.

4 Ibid.

5 See David Cramer, Jenny Howell, Jonathan Tran, and Paul Martens, "Scandalizing John Howard Yoder," *Other Journal: An Intersection of Theology & Culture*, 7 July 2014, https://theotherjournal.com/2014/07/07/scandalizing-john-howard-yoder; J. Denny Weaver, ed., *John Howard Yoder: Radical Theologian* (Eugene, OR: Cascade Books, 2014).

6 See Isaac Samuel Villegas, "The Ecclesial Ethics of John Howard Yoder's Abuse," *Modern Theology* 37, no. 1 (2021): 191–214; Lisa Schirch, "Afterword," in Weaver, *Radical Theologian*, 382; Carolyn Holderread Heggen, "Response," in *Peace Theology and Violence against Women*, ed. Elizabeth G. Yoder (Elkhart, IN: Institute of Mennonite Studies, 1992), 75; Susan Brooks Thistlethwaite, *Women's Bodies as Battlefield: Christian Theology and the Global War on Women* (New York: Palgrave

Macmillan, 2015), 157; Peter Dula, "Psychology, Ecclesiology and Yoder's Violence," *Mennonite Life* 68 (May 2014), https://mla.bethelks.edu/ml-archive/2014/psychology-ecclesiology-and-yoders-violence.php; Malinda E. Berry, "Avoiding Avoidance: Why I Assigned Body Politics This Spring," *Mennonite Life* 68 (May 2014), https://mla.bethelks.edu/ml-archive/2014/avoiding-avoidance-why-i-assigned-body-politics-th.php.

7 See Elizabeth Soto Albrecht and Darryl W. Stephens, eds, *Liberating the Politics of Jesus: Renewing Peace Theology through the Wisdom of Women* (New York: T&T Clark, 2020).

8 Ervin Stutzman, *From Nonresistance to Justice: The Transformation of Mennonite Church Peace Rhetoric 1908–2008* (Waterloo, ON: Herald Press, 2011), 90–6.

9 See John Howard Yoder, *The Christian Witness to the State* (Scottdale, PA: Herald Press, 2002), and Yoder, *The Politics of Jesus*, 2nd ed. (Grand Rapids, MI: William B. Eerdmans, 1994).

10 John Howard Yoder, *For the Nations: Essays Evangelical and Public* (Grand Rapids, MI: William B. Eerdmans, 1997), 222.

11 John Howard Yoder, *Body Politics: Five Practices of the Christian Community before the Watching World* (Scottdale, PA: Herald Press, 2001), ix.

12 John Howard Yoder, *The Royal Priesthood: Essays, Ecclesiological, and Ecumenical*, ed. Michael Cartwright (Grand Rapids, MI: William B. Eerdmans, 1994), 217–18.

13 Yoder, *For the Nations*, 179.

14 These are not the only practices, but he limited the discussion to five. And instead of focusing in communion and baptism, he chose other practices because he wanted to emphasize their importance as well. He did not want Christians to think that communion and baptism are the only important practices.

15 Yoder, *Body Politics*, 60.

16 Ibid., 70.

17 Yoder, *The Politics of Jesus*, 228–37.

18 John Roth, *Choosing against War: A Christian View* (Intercourse, PA: Good Books, 2002), 111–13.

19 Christian Early and Ted Grimsrud, eds, *A Pacifist Way of Knowing: John Howard Yoder's Nonviolence Epistemology* (Eugene, OR: Cascade Books, 2010), 137–54.

20 Yoder, *For the Nations*, 64.

21 Yoder does not explain fully what his understanding of reconciliation is. However, based on how he uses the term in *The Royal Priesthood*, it can be said that it involves working toward unity in a context marked by division, whether this division was caused by differences of belief, ethnicity, culture, race, or material possessions.

22 Yoder, *The Royal Priesthood*, 292.

23 Yoder, *For the Nations*, 8.

24 Yoder, *The Royal Priesthood*, 291.

25 Ibid., 223.

26 Ibid., 225.

27 Ibid., 230.

28 Ibid., 234.

29 Lois Barrett, "Defining Missional Church," in *Evangelical, Ecumenical, and Anabaptist Missiologies in Conversation*, ed. James Krabill, Walter Sawatsky, and Charles Van Engen (Maryknoll, NY: Orbis Books, 2006), 177.

30 My choice of "Northern America" here and elsewhere is a deliberate one, as I focus specifically in this book on the sub-region of North America comprising Canada and the United States. An account of Mennonite peoplehood in such places as Mexico, Central America, or the Caribbean (all considered parts of the North American continent in most standard definitions) is beyond the scope of the present analysis.

31 See Darrell L. Guder, ed., *Missional Church: A Vision for the Sending of the Church in North America* (Grand Rapids, MI: William B. Eerdmans, 1988).

32 It is important to note that Mennonite scholars were actively involved in the development of the concept of the missional church. For instance, Wilbert Shenk was part of the Gospel and Our Culture Network, Lois Barrett contributed a chapter to Guder's *Missional Church*, and in the process of shaping that book, they consulted with a few well-known theologians, including John Howard Yoder.

33 Wilbert Shenk, "Why Missional and Mennonite Should Make Perfect Sense," in *Fully Engaged: Missional Church in an Anabaptist Voice*, ed. Stanley Green and James Krabill (Kitchener, ON: Herald Press, 2015), 20–8.

34 Stanley Green, "From Engagement to Preservation and Back Again," in Green and Krabill, *Fully Engaged*, 32.

35 Ibid., 33.

36 The terms "Christendom" and "Constantinianism" are often used by Mennonite theologians and scholars. Christendom first occurred when the successors to Emperor Constantine officially chose Christianity as the official religion of the Roman Empire. As a result, from its position at the margins of society, the church became one of the dominant institutions and acquired immense political power and wealth. While the church enjoyed this position for several centuries in Europe, in modern times, one can no longer speak of Christendom. However, Mennonite scholars claim that the legacy and the mindset of Christendom still continue in our understanding of the church and mission. See Wilbert Shenk, ed., *The Transfiguration of Mission: Biblical, Theological, & Historical Foundations* (Waterloo, ON: Herald Press, 1993).

37 Lois Barrett, Darrell Guder, Walter Hobbs, George Hunsberger, Linford Stutzman, Jeff Kooten, and Dale Ziemer, *Treasure in Clay Jars: Patterns in Missional Faithfulness* (Grand Rapids, MI: William B. Eerdmans, 2004), ix–x.
38 Lois Barrett, "Missional Witness: The Church as Apostle to the World," in Guder, *Missional Church*, 114.
39 Ibid., 117–41.
40 Lois Barrett, "Resources and Supports for the Missional Church represented by Anabaptist-Mennonite History and Tradition" (paper presented at the Mennonite Historical Society, Elkhart, IN, Nov. 2005).
41 When Barrett writes about churches renouncing their Christendom mindset, she is specifically thinking about mainline rather than Mennonite churches. However, she explains that any church can be captive to this mentality, including Mennonite churches.
42 Barrett, "Defining Missional Church," 182.
43 Robert Suderman, *Re-imagining the Church: Implications of Being a People in the World*, ed. Andrew Gregory Suderman (Eugene, OR: Wipf & Stock, 2016), 54–5.
44 Robert Suderman, "Revisiting the Missional Church Vision: Where Are We Today?," *Canadian Mennonite* 8, no. 2 (2004): 6–8.
45 Lawrence Burkholder, *The Problem of Social Responsibility from the Perspective of the Mennonite Church* (Elkhart, IN: Institute of Mennonite Studies, 1989), 12.
46 Gordon Kaufman, *Nonresistance and Responsibility and Other Mennonite Essays* (Newton, KS: Faith and Life, 1979), 8–9, 64–5.
47 Duane Friesen, *Artists, Citizens, Philosophers: Seeking the Peace of the City* (Scottdale, PA: Herald Press, 2000), 67.
48 Ibid., 134.
49 Friesen sees too much individualism as problematic because it can lead to a life of isolation and a spiritual life and practices that are disconnected from one's church. He also sees too much collectivism in a church as dangerous because it can lead to a repressive environment in which one's identity is absorbed into that of the church, and the significance of individual persons and dignity are ignored. See Friesen, *Artists, Citizens, Philosophers*, 119.
50 Ibid., 163.
51 There are several focal practices, but they fall largely into four groups: rituals of moral formation (baptism, the Lord's Supper, Sabbath, prayer, and singing), process practices (the dialogical process of discernment, reconciliation, and recognition of gifts), pastoral care practices, and practices of service to the wider community (which address the needs of the world and hospitality).
52 Duane Friesen, "In Search of Security: A Theology and Ethic of Peace and Public Order," in *At Peace and Unafraid: Public Order, Security, and the Wisdom of*

the Cross, ed. Duane Friesen and Gerald Schlabach (Scottdale, PA: Herald Press, 2005), 42.

53 Ibid., 58.

54 Yoder, *The Royal Priesthood*, 17.

55 Malinda Elizabeth Berry, "Shalom Political Theology: A New Type of Mennonite Peace Theology for a New Era of Discipleship," *Conrad Grebel Review* 34, no. 1 (2016): 52.

56 Ibid., 51.

57 Malinda Elizabeth Berry, "This Mark of a Standing Human Figure Poised to Embrace: A Constructive Theology of Social Responsibility, Nonviolence & Nonconformity" (PhD diss., Union Theological Seminary, 2013), 93.

58 Willard Roth and Gerald Schlabach, eds, *Called Together to Be Peacemakers: Report of the International Dialogue between the Catholic Church and Mennonite World Conference 1998–2003* (Kitchener, ON: Pandora Press, 2005).

CHAPTER TWO

1 It is interesting to note how the "stakes" are identified slightly differently in these books. In *Mennonite Identity in Conflict*, Driedger identifies four of the Mennonite stakes as biblical theology, communities of believers, Germanic culture, and territorial land. See *Mennonite Identity in Conflict* (Lewiston, NY: E. Mellen, 1988), 38–9. In *Mennonite Mosaic*, Kauffman and Driedger perceive that the stakes are religious beliefs, understanding of community, concept of family, and institutions. See *Mennonite Mosaic: Identity and Modernization* (Scottdale, PA: Herald Press, 1991), 147. And in *Mennonite Peacemaking*, Driedger and Kraybill view the stakes as doctrinal beliefs, religious life, service to others, and ethnic culture. See *Mennonite Peacemaking: From Quietism to Activism* (Waterloo, ON: Herald Press, 1994), 175.

2 Kauffman and Driedger, *Mennonite Mosaic*, 67.

3 Calvin Redekop, *Mennonite Society* (Baltimore: Johns Hopkins University Press, 1989), 138.

4 Ibid., 89.

5 Frank Epp, *Mennonite Peoplehood: A Plea for New Initiative* (Waterloo, ON: Conrad Press, 1977), 96.

6 "Who Are the Mennonites?" Mennonite Historical Society of Canada, accessed 22 September 2020, https://mhsc.ca/who-are-the-mennonites/. I acknowledge Frank Epp's involvement in sexual misconduct, which has led me to use his work sparingly. For further details regarding these incidents, see "Investigation Reveals Misconduct by Influential Mennonite Leader," *Canadian Mennonite*,

28 May 2021, https://canadianmennonite.org/stories/investigation-reveals-misconduct-influential-mennonite-leader.

7 The Old Colony Mennonites of Manitoba, whose settlement goes back to 1789, expected that they would enjoy the same privileges they did in Russia, the privileges of exercising their religious principles and full autonomy in the education of their children. However, when the Canadian government passed the School Attendance Act in 1916, it required all private schools to conform to the standards established by the state. Despite several attempts to keep their "privilege," the Mennonites were no longer able to maintain autonomy over education, and so some left the country. See Cornelius Krahn and Leonard Sawatzky, "Old Colony Mennonites," *Global Anabaptist Mennonite Encyclopedia Online*, accessed 22 September 2020, https://gameo.org/index.php?title=Old_Colony_Mennonites.

8 "More about Mennonites," Mennonite Archival Image Database, accessed 22 September 2020, https://archives.mhsc.ca/More+about+Mennonites.

9 Frank H. Epp and Leo Driedger, "Mennonites," *Canadian Encyclopedia*, last modified 15 April 2015, https://www.thecanadianencyclopedia.ca/en/article/mennonites.

10 See T.D. Regehr, *Mennonites in Canada, 1939–1970: A People Transformed* (Toronto: University of Toronto, 1996).

11 Frank Epp, *Mennonites in Canada, 1920–1940: A People's Struggle for Survival* (Toronto: Macmillan, 1982), 510.

12 Regehr, *Mennonites in Canada*, 312.

13 Epp, *Mennonites in Canada*, 545.

14 Regehr, *Mennonites in Canada*, 418.

15 Samuel Steiner, *In Search of Promised Lands: A Religious History of Mennonites in Ontario* (Kitchener, ON: Herald Press, 2015), 589–93.

16 Regehr, *Mennonites in Canada*, 418.

17 Leo Driedger and Donald Kraybill, *Mennonite Peacemaking: From Quietism to Activism* (Scottdale, PA: Herald Press, 1994), 39.

18 Since this definition is widely accepted among Mennonite historians and sociologists, I simply echo it and continue with the discourse. Berger defines pluralism as a "social situation in which people with different ethnicities, worldviews, and moralities live together peacefully and interact with each other amicably." This interaction brings forward a situation in which relativization becomes a permanent experience, and as a result, it undermines several certainties and beliefs by which people used to live. See Peter Berger, *The Many Altars of Modernity: Toward a Paradigm for Religion in a Pluralist Age* (Boston: de Gruyter, 2014), 1–9.

19 Driedger and Kraybill, *Mennonite Peacemaking*, 47–8.

20 Ibid., 171–4.

21 Redekop, *Mennonite Society*, 268–9.

22 Ibid., 273.

23 "A Brief History of Mennonites in Canada," Mennonite Church Canada, accessed 22 June 2021, https://www.mennonitechurch.ca/about/history.

24 Adolf Ens, *Becoming a National Church: A History of the Conference of Mennonites in Canada* (Winnipeg: CMU Press, 2004), 177.

25 Ibid., 133–8.

26 Robert Suderman, *God's People Now! Face to Face with Mennonite Church Canada* (Waterloo, ON: Herald Press, 2007), 41.

27 Conrad Kanagy, *Road Signs for the Journey: A Profile of Mennonite Church USA* (Scottdale, PA: Herald Press, 2007), 52.

28 S.F. Pannabecker, Harold S. Bender, and Wilbert R. Shenk, "Mission (Missiology)," *Global Anabaptist Mennonite Encyclopedia Online*, accessed 31 May 2020, https://gameo.org/index.php?title=Mission_(Missiology)&oldid=167790; Redekop, *Mennonite Society*, 233.

29 Edmund Kaufman, *The Development of the Missionary and Philanthropic Interest among the Mennonites of North America* (Berne, IN: Mennonite Book Concern, 1931), 39.

30 Ibid., 56.

31 Regehr, *Mennonites in Canada*, 328; Wilbert Shenk, "The 'Great Century' Reconsidered," in *Anabaptism and Mission*, ed. Wilbert Shenk (Scottdale, PA: Herald Press, 1984), 162ff.

32 Redekop, *Mennonite Society*, 239.

33 Kaufman, *The Development of the Missionary and Philanthropic Interest among the Mennonites of North America*, 46; Redekop, *Mennonite Society*, 239.

34 See 2015 statistics available in the MWC World Directory, accessed 25 November 2019, https://mwc-cmm.org/sites/default/files/website_files/mwc_world_directory_2015_statistics.pdf.

35 Conrad Kanagy, Elizabeth Miller, and John D. Roth, *Global Anabaptist Profile: Belief and Practice in 24 Mennonite World Conference Churches* (Goshen, IN: Institute for the Study of Global Anabaptism, 2017), 29.

36 Robert Suderman asserts that about 84 per cent of all Mennonite World Church member churches are due to the direct missionary work of Mennonites of European descent. See Deborah Froese, "What's Up with Mennos and Mission?," *Canadian Mennonite*, 20 April 2016, https://canadianmennonite.org/stories/what%E2%80%99s-mennos-and-mission.

37 Redekop, *Mennonite Society*, 243.

38 Regehr, *Mennonites in Canada*, 330.

39 Ibid., 354.

40 Esther Epp-Tiessen, *Mennonite Central Committee in Canada: A History* (Winnipeg: CMU Press, 2013), 33–4.
41 Ibid., 79.
42 Regehr, *Mennonites in Canada*, 391.
43 Redekop, *Mennonite Society*, 253–4.
44 Epp-Tiessen, *Mennonite Central Committee in Canada*, 251–2.
45 Ibid., 266.
46 Whenever I use the term "Mennonite ethnicity," I am referring to Mennonites from Swiss, Dutch, German, and Russian cultural backgrounds, who are still the dominant group in Mennonite churches, both in Canada and in the United States.
47 Other marginalized Mennonite members have also faced exclusion. For more on these experiences, especially those of women and individuals who identify as LGBTQ2S+, see Cameron Altaras and Carol Penner, eds, *Resistance: Confronting Violence, Power, and Abuse within Peace Churches* (Elkhart, IN: Institute of Mennonite Studies, 2022).
48 In my email conversation with the executive minister of MC Canada, Doug Klassen, he shared that no qualitative or statistical research has been done on MC Canada, but based on the information he has gathered from church leaders across Canada, he estimates that around 20 per cent of MC Canada members are racialized or members of other ethnic churches. Klassen, email message to author, 22 February 2021. It is unfortunate that MC Canada has not done any statistical work to understand the extent of its racial and ethnic diversity. Statistics are important because they help leaders to work toward gender and racial equality and to ensure a fair share of resources are distributed among marginalized members. Without this kind of work, I am not sure how racial justice can be done within MC Canada's current structure.
49 Conrad Kanagy, *Road Signs for the Journey: A Profile of Mennonite Church USA* (Scottdale, PA: Herald Press, 2007), 64.
50 Ibid., 64.
51 See Duane Friesen and Gerald Schlabach, eds, *At Peace and Unafraid: Public Order, Security, and the Wisdom of the Cross* (Scottdale, PA: Herald Press, 2005).

PART TWO

1 My liberative approach has been inspired and informed by liberation theologies, but it is not rooted in the work of these theologies. My approach seeks personal, communal, and social transformation based on love, justice, and shalom, liberating people from unloving and unjust systems of control in order to create shalom.

CHAPTER THREE

1 Angie Pears, *Doing Contextual Theology* (New York: Routledge, 2010), 1.

2 This does not mean that all views acknowledging that theologies are not fixed, universal, or objective are free from oppression or violence. However, from a contextual theological perspective, recognizing these features is crucial to any constructive dialogue and engagement with theologies from different contexts.

3 Sigurd Bergmann, *God in Context: A Survey of Contextual Theology* (Burlington, VT: Ashgate, 2003), 2.

4 Stephen Bevans, *Models of Contextual Theology*, rev. and expanded ed. (Maryknoll, NY: Orbis Books, 2002), 4.

5 Walter Hollenweger, "Intercultural Theology: Some Remarks on the Term," in *Towards an Intercultural Theology: Essays in Honor of J. A. B. Jongeneel*, ed. Martha Fredriks, Meindert Dijkstra, and Anton Hontepen (Zoetermer, NL: Uitgeverij Meinema, 2003), 90–1.

6 Bergmann, *God in Context*, 44.

7 Bevans, *Models of Contextual Theology*, 5–6.

8 Néstor Medina, *Christianity, Empire, and the Spirit: (Re)Configuring Faith and the Cultural* (Boston: Brill, 2018), 2.

9 Kathryn Tanner, *Theories of Culture: A New Agenda for Theology* (Minneapolis, MN: Augsburg Fortress, 1997), 3–24.

10 T.J. Gorringe, *Furthering Humanity: A Theology of Culture* (Burlington, VT: Ashgate, 2004), 3–9.

11 Tanner, *Theories of Culture*, 25–8.

12 Ibid., 39.

13 Ibid.

14 Ibid., 57.

15 Ibid., 57–8.

16 Medina, *Christianity, Empire, and the Spirit*, 32.

17 Gorringe, *Furthering Humanity*, 105.

18 Ibid., 149.

19 Ibid., 130.

20 Ibid.

21 James Neuliep, *Intercultural Communication: A Contextual Approach*, 8th ed. (Thousand Oaks, CA: Sage Publications, 2021), 87.

22 Paul Bramadat, "Beyond Christian Canada: Religion and Ethnicity in a Multicultural Society," in *Religion and Ethnicity in Canada*, ed. Paul Bramadat and David Seljak (Toronto: University of Toronto Press, 2009), 8.

23 Royden Loewen, "The Poetics of Peoplehood: Ethnicity and Religion among Canada's Mennonites" in *Christianity and Ethnicity in Canada*, ed. Paul Bramadat and David Seljak (Toronto: University of Toronto Press, 2008), 332.
24 Vic Satzewich and Nikolaos Liodakis, *"Race" and Ethnicity in Canada: A Critical Introduction*, 4th ed. (Toronto: Oxford University Press, 2017), 6.
25 Ibid., 6.
26 Bramadat, "Beyond Christian Canada," 24.
27 Michael Banton, *Racial Theories*, 2nd ed. (Cambridge: Cambridge University Press, 1998), 5–8.
28 Carl James, *Seeing Ourselves: Exploring Race, Ethnicity and Culture* (Toronto: Thompson Educational, 2010), 40.
29 Ibid., 136.
30 Ibid., 137.
31 Kathy Hogarth and Wendy Fletcher, *A Space for Race: Decoding Racism, Multiculturalism, and Post-colonialism in the Quest for Belonging in Canada and Beyond* (New York: Oxford University Press, 2018), 6.
32 Özlem Sensoy and Robin DiAngelo, *Is Everyone Really Equal? An Introduction to Key Concepts in Social Justice Education*, 2nd ed. (New York: Teachers College Press, Columbia University, 2017), 241.
33 Robin DiAngelo, *White Fragility: Why It's so Hard for White People to Talk about Racism* (Boston: Beacon Press, 2018), 89–90.
34 Ibid.
35 Ibid., 19.
36 Bevans, *Models of Contextual Theology*, 31.
37 Ibid., 104.
38 Stephen Bevans, *An Introduction to Theology in Global Perspective* (Maryknoll, NY: Orbis Books, 2009), 182.
39 Bevans, *Models of Contextual Theology*, 141–3.
40 Ibid., 39–40.
41 Gorringe, *Furthering Humanity*, 213.
42 Ibid.

CHAPTER FOUR

1 Ruth Mojeed, "The Black Experience in Multicultural Canada," *Douglas Magazine*, 10 June 2020, https://www.douglasmagazine.com/the-black-experience-in-multicultural-canada.
2 Ibid.
3 Augie Fleras and Jean Leonard Elliott, *Engaging Diversity: Multiculturalism in Canada* (Toronto: Thompson Educational, 2002), 66–7.

4 Canadian Multiculturalism Act, RSC 1985, c. 24 (4th Supp.).

5 Ibid.

6 Sunera Thobani, *Exalted Subjects: Studies in the Making of Race and Nation in Canada* (Toronto: University of Toronto Press, 2007), 8.

7 Young, *Justice and the Politics of Difference*, 41.

8 Ibid., 39–65.

9 Himani Bannerji, *The Dark Side of the Nation: Essays on Multiculturalism, Nationalism, and Gender* (Toronto: Canadian Scholars' Press, 2000), 9–10.

10 Carl James, *Seeing Ourselves: Exploring Race, Ethnicity and Culture* (Toronto: Thompson Educational, 2010), 210.

11 Fleras and Elliott, *Engaging Diversity*, 42.

12 Rita Dhamoon, *Identity/Difference Politics: How Difference Is Produced, and Why It Matters* (Vancouver: UBC Press, 2009), x.

13 Bannerji, *The Dark Side of the Nation*, 92–3.

14 Fleras and Elliott, *Engaging Diversity*, 19.

15 See Kimberlé Crenshaw, "Mapping the Margins: Intersectionality, Identity Politics, and Violence against Women of Colour," in *The Public Nature of Private Violence*, ed. M.A. Fineman and R. Mykitiul (New York: Routledge, 1995), 93–120.

16 Kathy Hogarth and Wendy Fletcher, *A Space for Race: Decoding Racism, Multiculturalism, and Post-colonialism in the Quest for Belonging in Canada and Beyond* (New York: Oxford University Press, 2018), 90.

17 See Susan Moller Okin, *Is Multiculturalism Bad for Women?* (Princeton, NJ: Princeton University Press, 1999).

18 Sneja Gunew, *Haunted Nations: The Colonial Dimensions of Multiculturalisms* (New York: Routledge, 2004), 40–1.

19 Hogarth and Fletcher, *A Space for Race*, 92–3.

20 Bannerji, *The Dark Side of the Nation*, 81.

21 Emma Battell Lowman and Adam J. Barker, *Settler: Identity and Colonialism in 21st Century Canada* (Winnipeg: Fernwood, 2015), 116–20.

22 Alain-G. Gagnon and Raffaele Iacovino, "Interculturalism and Multiculturalism: Similarities and Differences," in *Multiculturalism and Interculturalism: Debating the Divided Lines*, ed. Nasar Meer, Tariq Modood, and Ricard Zapata-Barrero (Edinburgh: Edinburgh University Press, 2016), 111–15.

23 Dimitrios Karmis, "Pluralism and National Identity(ies) in Contemporary Quebec: Conceptual Clarifications, Typology, and Discourse Analysis," in *Québec: State & Society*, ed. Alain-G. Gagnon, 3rd ed. (Peterborough, ON: Broadview Press, 2004), 79–80.

24 See "Our History," TIM Centre, Tyndale University, accessed 11 June 2024, https://www.tyndale.ca/tim/about/history.

25 Rob Fennell, ed., *Intercultural Visions: Called to Be the Church* (Toronto: United Church House, 2012), 1.

26 See "Being Multicultural, Becoming Intercultural – Executive Summary," Anglican Diocese of Toronto, 29 September 2011, https://www.toronto.anglican.ca/uploads.php?id=4f9eb730ca533.

27 See "The History of the Forum for Intercultural Leadership and Learning," Canadian Council of Churches, accessed 11 June 2024, https://www.intercultural leadership.ca/our-history/.

28 Robert J. Schreiter, "Teaching Theology from an Intercultural Perspective," *Theological Education* 26, no. 1 (1989): 19.

29 "Definition" is in quotation marks to indicate that my definition of interculturality is not exhaustive or universal; interculturality is a contested concept, and it is still evolving. However, to help readers focus and to avoid any confusion, I offer a brief and tentative explanation of the term.

30 Anthony Gittins, "The Challenge of Intercultural Living: Anthropological and Theological Implications," in *Intercultural Living: Explorations in Missiology*, ed. Lazar Stanislaus and Martin Ueffing (Maryknoll, NY: Orbis Books, 2018), 2.

31 Olga Consuelo Vélez Caro, "Toward a Feminist Intercultural Theology," in *Feminist Intercultural Theology: Latina Explorations for a Just World*, ed. María Pilar Aquino and María José Rosado-Nunes (Maryknoll, NY: Orbis Books, 2007), 253.

32 Henning Wrogemann, *Intercultural Theology*, vol. 2, *Theologies of Mission*, trans. Karl Bohmer (Downers Grove, IL: InterVarsity Press), 336.

33 Theo Sundermeier, "My Pilgrimage in Mission," *International Bulletin of Missionary Research* 31, no. 4 (2007): 201.

34 Wrogemann, *Theologies of Mission*, 336.

35 Leonardo Boff, *Virtues: For Another Possible World* (Eugene, OR: Cascade Books, 2011), 72–3. "Relativize" is a slippery term because by relativizing the differences, we can too quickly move to "common ground" and gloss over or minimize difference. Yet, in Boff's writing, he is using the term not to minimize the difference, but rather to avoid absolutizing and/or overemphasizing difference to such an extent that there can be no co-living or relating with one another.

36 Raúl Fornet-Betancourt, *Filosofar para Nuestro Tiempo en Clave Intercultural*, vol. 1 (Aachen, DE: Mainz, 2004), 41.

37 Raúl Fornet-Betancourt, *Interculturalidad y globalización: Ejercicios de crítica filosófica intercultural en el contexto de la globalización neoliberal* (San Jose, CR: Editorial DEI, 2000), 85.

38 Ibid., 85.

39 Perry Yoder, *Shalom: The Bible's Word for Salvation, Justice, & Peace* (Nappanee, IN: Evangel Publishing, 1987), 13.

40 Ibid., 16.

41 Ibid., 16–18.
42 Ibid., 39–49.
43 T.J. Gorringe, *Furthering Humanity: A Theology of Culture* (Burlington, VT: Ashgate, 2004), 149.

CHAPTER FIVE

1 See "The Schleitheim Confession of Faith," *Mennonite Quarterly Review* 19, no. 4 (1945): 247–53.
2 Historically and traditionally, this separation has been emphasized in the Mennonite belief in nonresistance and nonconformity. See Leo Driedger and Donald Kraybill, *Mennonite Peacemaking: From Quietism to Activism* (Scottdale, PA: Herald Press, 1994), 49; Ervin Stutzman, *From Nonresistance to Justice: The Transformation of Mennonite Church Peace Rhetoric 1908–2008* (Waterloo, ON: Herald Press, 2011), 40–1.
3 Emily Ralph Servant, "The Gentrification of the Margins," *Mennonite Quarterly Review* 92, no. 3 (2018): 405.
4 John Howard Yoder, *The Royal Priesthood: Essays, Ecclesiological, and Ecumenical*, ed. Michael Cartwright (Grand Rapids, MI: William B. Eerdmans, 1994), 224.
5 General Conference Mennonite Church and Mennonite Church, *Confession of Faith in a Mennonite Perspective* (Scottdale, PA: Herald Press, 1995), 21–2.
6 See Howard Loewen, *One Lord, One Church, One Hope, and One God: Mennonite Confessions of Faith* (Elkhart, IN: Institute of Mennonite Studies, 1985), 47–8.
7 Yoder, *The Royal Priesthood*, 353.
8 See John Howard Yoder, *A Pacifist Way of Knowing: John Howard Yoder's Nonviolent Epistemology* (Eugene, OR: Cascade Books, 2010), 40–57.
9 John Howard Yoder, "How H. Richard Niebuhr Reasoned: A Critique of Christ and Culture," in *Authentic Transformation: A New Vision of Christ and Culture*, ed. Glen Stassen, D.M. Yeager, and John Howard Yoder (Nashville, TN: Abingdon Press), 79.
10 Daniel Schipani, "Liberation Theologies," *Global Anabaptist Mennonite Encyclopedia Online*, accessed 7 January 2021, https://gameo.org/index.php?title=Liberation_Theologies.
11 It is interesting to observe that even though Schipani is from Argentina, received several degrees from Argentina, taught extensively in Puerto Rico, and served as a co-editor of the book *Through the Eyes of Another: Intercultural Reading of the Bible* (Elkhart, IN: Institute of Mennonite Studies, 2004), he seems unaware of how social locations influence theologies. This is a good reminder that even though one has diverse cultural backgrounds and cross-cultural experiences,

they do not automatically place one in a position to comprehend how context shapes one's faith.

12 Fernando Enns, "Believers Church Ecclesiology: A Trinitarian Foundation and Its Implications," in *New Perspectives in Believers Church Ecclesiology*, ed. Abe Dueck, Helmut Harder, and Karl Koop (Winnipeg: CMU Press, 2010), 187.

13 For other exceptional Mennonite scholars who incorporate a Trinitarian view, see A. James Reimer, *Mennonites and Classical Theology: Foundations for Christian Ethics* (Kitchener, ON: Pandora Press, 2001); Thomas Finger, *A Contemporary Anabaptist Theology* (Downers Grove, IL: InterVarsity Press, 2004); and Arnold Neufeld-Fast, "Examining the Believers Church within a Trinitarian-Missional Framework," in Dueck, Harder, and Koop, *New Perspectives in Believers Church Ecclesiology*.

14 Lydia Harder, *Obedience, Suspicion, and the Gospel of Mark: A Mennonite-Feminist Exploration of Biblical Authority* (Waterloo, ON: Wilfrid Laurier University Press, 1998), 38–9.

15 Tobin Shearer, "Conflicting Identities: White Racial Formation among Mennonites, 1960–1985," *Identities: Global Studies in Culture and Power* 19, no. 3 (2012): 268.

16 Jill Stoltzfus, "Awareness of Being White, Perceptions about Racial Minority Groups, and Interracial Contact: A Study of Mennonites in America" (PhD diss., University of Pennsylvania, 1999), 5.

17 Malinda Berry, "On Racism, Mennonite Politics, and Liberation: Words We Don't Like to Hear," *Vision: A Journal for Church and Theology* 3 (Fall 2002): 24.

18 Sara Ahmed, "A Phenomenology of Whiteness," *Feminist Theory* 8 (2007): 157.

19 Özlem Sensoy and Robin DiAngelo, *Is Everyone Really Equal? An Introduction to Key Concepts in Social Justice Education*, 2nd ed. (New York: Teachers College Press, Columbia University, 2017), 122.

20 Jennifer Harvey, *Dear White Christians: For Those Still Longing for Racial Reconciliation* (Grand Rapids, MI: William B. Eerdmans, 2014), 77.

21 Ibid., 77.

22 See Vincent Harding, *The Task of the Mennonite Church in Establishing Racial Unity* (Goshen, IN: Woodlawn Mennonite Church, 1959). This was the time when Mennonite churches in Canada were directly connected with Mennonite churches in the United States through the General Conference Mennonite Church.

23 See Felipe Hinojosa, *Latino Mennonites: Civil Rights, Faith & Evangelical Culture* (Baltimore: Johns Hopkins University Press, 2014).

24 Tobin Shearer, "State of the Race: A Short History of Mennonite Racial Statements, 1940–1979," *Anabaptist Historians: Bringing the Anabaptist Past into a*

Digital Century, 3 October 2019, https://anabaptisthistorians.org/2019/10/03/state-of-the-race-a-short-history-of-mennonite-racial-statements-1940-1979.

25 Shearer, "Conflicting Identities," 276.

26 I would prefer to use a term other than "racially colour-blind," because the terms "blind" and "blindness" have often been used in a manner derogatory to people with visual disabilities. Yet if I do not use this term, readers might not understand my argument. I therefore use it only when I discuss racism. Informed by dis/ability theologies, in all my writing I intentionally avoid using the terms "blind," "blindness," "deaf," and "deafness" to refer someone as unlearned or immature, because these disabilities do not directly cause a person to be ignorant.

27 Jeffrey Phillip Gingerich, "Sharing the Faith: Racial and Ethnic Identity in an Urban Mennonite Community" (PhD diss., University of Pennsylvania, 2003), 203.

28 Ibid., 203.

29 Traci West, *Disruptive Christian Ethics: When Racism and Women's Lives Matter* (Louisville, KY: Westminster John Knox Press, 2006), 118.

30 Ibid., 119.

31 This expression is found in Ephesians 5:27, addressing the pure relationship between husbands and wives within Christian households. Historically, Mennonites have embraced this image to emphasize the message that newly born Christians are called to live as a community free from moral failure. See Karl Koop and Mary Schertz, *Without Spot or Wrinkle: Reflecting Theologically on the Nature of the Church* (Elkhart, IN: Institute of Mennonite Studies, 2000).

32 Although it is not actively and widely practised, shunning, banning, or excommunicating were historical practices of the Mennonites from as early as the sixteenth century. See John Enger, "Avoidance," *Global Anabaptist Mennonite Encyclopedia Online*, accessed 21 May 2021, https://gameo.org/index.php?title=Avoidance.

33 Richard Gula, *What Are They Saying about Moral Norms?* (New York: Paulist Press, 1982), 1.

34 Marlene Epp, *Mennonite Women in Canada: A History* (Winnipeg: University of Manitoba Press, 2008), 184.

35 Lydia Harder, *Obedience, Suspicion, and the Gospel of Mark: A Mennonite-Feminist Exploration of Biblical Authority* (Waterloo, ON: Wilfrid Laurier University Press, 1998), 38–9.

36 Cathy Ross, "Hospitality: The Church as 'A Mother with an Open Heart,'" in *Mission on the Road to Emmaus: Constants, Context, and Prophetic Dialogue*, ed. Cathy Ross and Stephen Bevans (Maryknoll, NY: Orbis Books, 2015), 69.

37 Christine Pohl, *Making Room: Recovering Hospitality as a Christian Tradition* (Grand Rapids, MI: William B. Eerdmans, 1999), 17.

38 Thomas Reynolds, "Beyond Hospitality? Unsettling Theology and Migration in Canada," in *Religion and Migration: Negotiating Hospitality, Agency and Vulnerability*, ed. Andrea Bieler, Isolde Karle, HyeRan Kim-Cragg, and Ilona Nord (Leipzig, DE: Evangelische Verlagsanstalt, 2019), 115.

39 Ibid., 118.

40 Letty Russell, *Just Hospitality: God's Welcome in a World of Difference* (Louisville, KY: Westminster John Knox Press, 2009), 105.

41 Ibid., 106.

42 Cathy Ross, "Hospitality: The Church as 'a Mother with an Open Heart,'" in Ross and Bevans, *Mission on the Road to Emmaus*, 70.

43 John Howard Yoder, *Body Politics: Five Practices of the Christian Community before the Watching World* (Scottdale, PA: Herald Press, 2001), 60.

44 Farley, *Just Love*, 197.

45 Dawn Nothwehr, *Mutuality: A Formal Norm for Christian Social Ethics* (Eugene, OR: Wipf & Stock, 2005), 17.

46 See Daniel C. Maguire, *The Moral Core of Judaism and Christianity* (Minneapolis, MN: Fortress Press, 1993), 165; Christopher D. Marshall, *The Little Book of Biblical Justice: A Fresh Approach to the Bible's Teachings on Justice* (Intercourse, PA: Good Books, 2005), 65–6; David P. Gushee and Glen H. Stassen, *Kingdom Ethics: Following Jesus in Contemporary Context*, 2nd ed. (Grand Rapid, MI: William B. Eerdmans, 2016), 87–92.

47 Farley, *Just Love*, 196–206.

48 Marvin Ellison, *Keeping Body and Soul Together: Sexuality, Spirituality, and Social Justice* (Louisville, KY: Office of the General Assembly, 1991), 9.

49 Marilyn Legge, "'In the Company of God and One Another': Feminist Theo-ethics, Heterogeneous Publics and Intercultural Churches," in *Public Theology and the Challenge of Feminism*, ed. Stephen Burns and Anita Monro (New York: Routledge, 2015), 47.

50 María Pilar Aquino, "Feminist Intercultural Theology," in *Feminist Intercultural Theology: Latina Explorations for a Just World*, ed. María Pilar and Maria José Rosado-Nunes (Maryknoll, NY: Orbis Books, 2007), 16.

51 Leo Driedger and Donald Kraybill, *Mennonite Peacemaking: From Quietism to Activism* (Scottdale, PA: Herald Press, 1994), 87.

52 Ibid., 151–2; Ervin Stutzman, *From Nonresistance to Justice: The Transformation of Mennonite Church Peace Rhetoric 1908–2008* (Waterloo, ON: Herald Press, 2011), 183–210.

53 Dawn Nothwehr, "Mutuality and Mission: A No 'Other' Way," *Mission Studies* 21, no. 2 (2004): 260.

54 Ibid., 254.

55 See Yoder, *The Royal Priesthood.*

56 Calvin Redekop, "Power in the Anabaptist Community," in *Power, Authority, and the Anabaptist Tradition*, ed. Benjamin Redekop and Calvin Redekop (Baltimore: Johns Hopkins University Press, 2001), 187.

57 Fernando Enns and Helmut Harder, *The Peace Church and The Ecumenical Community: Ecclesiology and the Ethics of Nonviolence* (Kitchener, ON: Pandora Press/World Council of Churches Publications, 2007), 232.

58 Ibid., 232.

CHAPTER SIX

1 Christen Kong, email message to author, 19 October 2023.

2 John Howard Yoder, *Body Politics: Five Practices of the Christian Community before the Watching World* (Scottdale, PA: Herald Press, 2001), 30; Larry Miller, "The Church as Messianic Society," in *The Transfiguration of Mission: Biblical, Theological, & Historical Foundations*, ed. Wilber Shenk (Waterloo, ON: Herald Press, 2993), 137.

3 John Howard Yoder, *The Royal Priesthood: Essays, Ecclesiological, and Ecumenical*, ed. Michael Cartwright (Grand Rapids, MI: William B. Eerdmans, 1994), 292.

4 There is real concern among more marginalized groups that by shifting social, racial, and ethnic identities, they might lose what they value and respect. For this reason, these groups resist change, and rightly so. In this case, it is important that the groups decide if they prefer to change, and it is fitting if they choose a strategic essentialism approach. This means that although there are no essentialist features or generalized representations in the identity of a social group, people from that particular group can uphold some features as essential for the sake of solidarity and social transformation, while being mindful that these features and representations are provisional and open to change.

5 Forum for Intercultural Leadership and Learning, "Intercultural Leadership and Learning Workshop," Canadian Council of Churches Governing Board, 28 November 2019. Printed material in the author's possession. The chart has been adapted from Crossroads Ministry continuum, which is based on the Jackson and Hardiman model and the Bennett development model of intercultural sensitivity. See Rita Hardiman and Bailey Jackson, "Conceptual Foundations for Social Justice Education Conceptual Overview," in *Teaching for Diversity and Social Justice*, ed. Maurianne Adams, Lee Anne Bell, and Pat Griffin, 2nd ed. (New York: Routledge, 2007), and Milton J. Bennett, "Development Model of Intercultural Sensitivity," in *International Encyclopedia of Intercultural Communication*, ed. Kim Young Yun (Hoboken, NJ: John Wiley and Sons, 2017).

6 Charles Kraft, *Christianity in Culture: A Study in Biblical Theologizing in Cross-Cultural Perspective* (Maryknoll, NY: Orbis Books, 2005), 230.

7 Hyung Jin Kim Sun, "Intercultural Global Theology," *Vision: A Journal for Church and Theology* 19, no. 2 (2018): 86–8. Robert Schreiter coined the concept "theological global flows" and named the four flows as liberation, feminism, ecology, and human rights. However, in my article "Intercultural Global Theology," I add a fifth one, which is peace/reconciliation. Schreiter intentionally chose the word "flow" to indicate that these themes are not uniform or systemic but instead "represent a series of linked, mutually intelligible discourses that address the contradictions or failures of global systems" (16). Moreover, these flows are not to be seen as universal themes from an Enlightenment perspective, but rather as themes found all over the world and affecting almost everyone. See Robert Schreiter, *The New Catholicity: Theology between the Global and the Local* (Maryknoll, NY: Orbis Books, 1997), 16–20.

8 Timothy Epp, "Blackness, Whiteness, and the Anabaptist Imagined Community in Print and Mission," *Conrad Grebel Review* 39, no. 3 (2021): 263–4.

9 Malinda Berry, "On Racism, Mennonite Politics, and Liberation: Words We Don't Like to Hear," *Vision: A Journal for Church and Theology* 3 (Fall 2002): 24.

10 "PRRI Survey: Friendship Networks of White Americans Continue to Be 90% White," Public Religion Research Institute, 24 May 2022, https://www.prri.org/press-release/prri-survey-friendship-networks-of-white-americans-continue-to-be-90-white.

11 Maire Sinha, *Canadians' Connections with Family and Friends*, Statistics Canada, Catalogue No. 89652X – No. 006 (Ottawa: Minister of Industry, 2014), https://www150.statcan.gc.ca/n1/en/catalogue/89-652-X2014006.

12 Mennonite Church Executive Board, "Mennonite Church USA Statement on Racial Injustice," Mennonite Church USA, 1 June 2020, http://mennoniteusa.org/news/mc_usa-statement-on-racial-injustice.

13 Executive Staff Group of Mennonite Church Canada, "Nationwide Call to Prayer for Sunday, 7 June 2020: Regional Churches of Mennonite Church Canada to Join Mennonite Church USA in Prayer of Lament over Injustice," Mennonite Church Canada, 3 June 2020, https://www.mennonitechurch.ca/news/10380-nationwide-call-to-prayer-for-sunday-june-7-2020.

14 I am aware of the sexual misconduct of John Rempel, and so I only utilize his work in a limited way. To learn more about this misconduct, see "Statement Concerning Incidents of Historical Sexual Misconduct," Conrad Grebel University College, University of Waterloo, 20 October 2020, https://uwaterloo.ca/grebel/historic-sexual-misconduct.

15 John Rempel, "The Lord's Supper in Mennonite Tradition," *Vision: A Journal for Church and Theology* 2, no. 1 (2001): 15.

16 See Eleanor Kreider, "Communion as Storytime," *Vision: A Journal for Church and Theology* 2, no. 1 (2001): 16–27.

17 Alan Kreider and Eleanor Kreider, *Worship and Mission: After Christendom* (Waterloo, ON: Herald Press, 2011), 251–5.

18 Eleanor Kreider, *Communion Shapes Character* (Scottdale, PA: Herald Press, 1997), 190–5.

19 Stephanie Spellers, "Introduction to the 15th Anniversary Edition," in *Radical Welcome: Embracing God, the Other and the Spirit of Transformation*, 15th anniv. ed. (New York: Morehouse Publishing, 2021), xvi.

20 Stephanie Spellers, *Radical Welcome: Embracing God, the Other, and the Spirit of Transformation* (New York: Church Publishing, 2006), 64.

21 Spellers, "Bread for the Journey."

22 Spellers, *Radical Welcome*, 20.

23 See Stephen Bevans and Roger Schroeder, *Constants in Context: Theology of Mission for Today* (Maryknoll, NY: Orbis Books, 2004).

24 Cathy Ross and Stephen Bevans, "Introduction," in *Mission on the Road to Emmaus: Constants, Context, and Prophetic Dialogue*, ed. Cathy Ross and Stephen Bevans (Maryknoll, NY: Orbis Books, 2015), xi.

25 Ibid. xii.

26 Ibid., xiv.

27 See Johan Galtung, "Violence, Peace, and Peace Research," *Journal of Peace Research* 6, no. 3 (1969): 167–91.

28 Cynthia Moe-Lobeda, *Resisting Structural Evil: Love as Ecological-Economic Vocation* (Minneapolis, MN: Fortress Press, 2013), 72.

29 Galtung, "Violence, Peace, and Peace Research," 291.

30 Jennifer Harvey, *Dear White Christians: For Those Still Longing for Racial Reconciliation* (Grand Rapids, MI: Eerdmans Publishing Company, 2014), 86.

31 Ibid., 86.

32 Truth and Reconciliation Commission of Canada, *Honouring the Truth, Reconciling for the Future: Summary of the Final Report of the Truth and Reconciliation Commission of Canada* (Winnipeg: Truth and Reconciliation Commission of Canada, 2015), 14.

33 Ibid., 184.

34 Jeremy M. Bergen, "Whether, and How, a Church Ought to Repent for a Historical Wrong," *Theology Today* 73, no. 2 (2016): 135.

35 Ibid.

36 Ibid., 136.

37 Marilyn Legge, "In the Company of God and One Another: Feminist Theo-ethics, Heterogeneous Publics and Intercultural Churches," in *Public Theology and the*

Challenge of Feminism, ed. Anita Monro and Stephen Burns (New York: Routledge, 2015), 54.

38 John Paul Lederach, *Moral Imagination: The Art and Soul of Building Peace* (New York: Oxford University Press, 2005), 30.

39 Emma Battell Lowman and Adam J. Barker, *Settler: Identity and Colonialism in 21st Century Canada* (Winnipeg: Fernwood, 2015), 64.

40 Adrian Jacobs, "The First Covenant," *Do Justice*, 9 January 2023, https://dojustice.crcna.org/article/first-covenant.

41 Rachel Bergen, "Mennonites Advocate for Bill C-262," *Canadian Mennonite*, 10 April 2019, https://canadianmennonite.org/c262-rally.

42 Katie Doke Sawatzky, "New Anthology Documents Six Decades of Anabaptist Response to Indigenous Calls for Justice," Mennonite Church Canada, 21 September 2020, https://www.mennonitechurch.ca/article/10700-new-anthology-documents-six-decades-of-anabaptist-response-to-indigenous-calls-for-justice; Steve Heinrichs and Esther Epp-Thiessen, eds, *Be It Resolved: Anabaptists & Partner Coalitions Advocate for Indigenous Justice* (Winnipeg: Mennonite Church Canada, 2020).

CONCLUSION

1 Sofia Samatar, *The White Mosque: A Memoir* (New York: Catapult, 2022), 292–3.

2 Ibid., 262.

3 Ibid., 263.

INDEX